PACIFIC MARINE FISHES

WARREN BURGESS & DR. HERBERT R. AXELROD

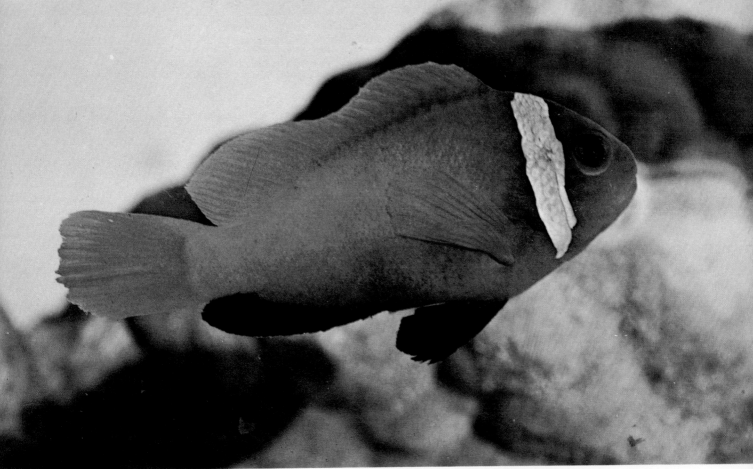

1. *Amphiprion nigripes* Regan. This anemonefish is found only at the Maldive Islands in the Indian Ocean. Photo by Dr. Herbert R. Axelrod.

Book 3

FISHES OF SRI LANKA, (CEYLON), THE MALDIVE ISLANDS AND MOMBASA.

Distributed in the U.S.A. by T.F.H. Publications, Inc., 211 West Sylvania
Avenue, P.O. Box 27, Neptune City, N.J. 07753; in England by T.F.H.
(Gt. Britain) Ltd., 13 Nutley Lane, Reigate, Surrey; in Canada by Clarke,
Irwin & Company, Clarwin House, 791 St. Clair Avenue West, Toronto
10, Ontario; in Southeast Asia by Y. W. Ong, 9 Lorong 36 Geylang,
Singapore 14; in Australia and the south Pacific by Pet Imports Pty.
Ltd., P.O. Box 149, Brookvale 2100, N.S.W., Australia.
Published by T.F.H. Publications, Inc. Ltd., The British Crown Colony of
Hong Kong.

TABLE OF CONTENTS

Because of the difficulty and attendant great cost involved in the typography work necessary to repro- duce diacritical marks normally used only with foreign languages, we have begun in this volume of *Pacific Marine Fishes* to reproduce without diacritical marks the names of those foreign ichthyologists whose names in exact correctness are rendered with appropriate non-English diacritical marks. Lacépède, Günther and Forskål, for example, will in this and succeeding volumes appear as Lacepede, Gunther and Forskal. The purpose of this move is, of course, to effect economies of production that will allow the publishers to continue to offer the *Pacific Marine Fishes* series at no increase in cost over the original volumes.

FISHES OF SRI LANKA, (CEYLON), THE MALDIVE ISLANDS AND MOMBASA.

INTRODUCTION

In Books 1 and 2 of this series the fishes presented were almost exclusively from parts of the Pacific Ocean. More specifically, the majority were from Japanese coastal waters, especially those around islands such as Okinawa. In this the third book we are expanding our coverage of the fishes to include the Indian Ocean. Succeeding books will hopefully deal with specific geographic areas such as Taiwan, Australia, the Red Sea, Hawaii, Philippines, etc. All these areas form part of the vast Indo-Pacific fauna region of zoogeographers, which roughly delimits the scope of this series of books.

Two very important collecting areas were visited by one of the authors (HRA) to photograph the fishes for this book. The first was the Maldive Islands, which are situated west and south of the southern tip of India and Sri Lanka (Ceylon) in the central part of the Indian Ocean. The second area visited was Mombasa, on the eastern coast of Africa in the western part of the Indian Ocean. Rodney Jonklaas aided in the capture and photography of the fishes of the Maldive Islands and provided additional photographs from Sri Lanka, his home diving territory. Ray Allard provided similar help in the Mombasa area and also, provided photographs of different species of fishes he was able to collect recently.

Some of the species presented here have appeared in the earlier books of this series. If the reader looks closely, however, he may detect some differences between the Pacific Ocean and Indian Ocean forms of the same species. In the geologic past, when the levels of the oceans were lower, there was a land barrier between the two oceans, the remnants of which can presently be seen as the Indo-Australian Archipelago composed of such islands as Java, Sumatra, etc. The separation of the faunas of the two oceans apparently allowed evolutionary forces to differentiate between certain homologous species on either side of the barrier. It is the interpretation of these differences that may cause problems for taxonomists. Where one might be of the opinion that the differences are significant enough to call the two forms distinct species, another might regard the same two forms as subspecies (or even identical species!). The photographs in this book should be compared with those from Books 1 and 2 to appreciate those differences which have evolved among the fishes of these two areas.

Many of the species in this book are represented by color photographs for the first time. In many cases juvenile forms that have never been seen before are also included.

Many of the fishes photographed by Allard and Axelrod in Mombasa were preserved and the specimens deposited at the USNM in Washington for further reference. An additional objective of the authors is to make photographs of living fishes, preserve these identical fishes, and have them available for study at recognized museums. This is, of course, only practical when specimens are collected and photographed in special aquaria or photographic trays.

2. The sparkling clear waters of the Maldive Islands off the southwest coast of India were the source for many of the fishes pictured in this book. Photo by Dr. Herbert R. Axelrod.

The sparkling waters of the Islands off the coast of Mombasa.　Photo by Dr. Herbert R. Axelrod.

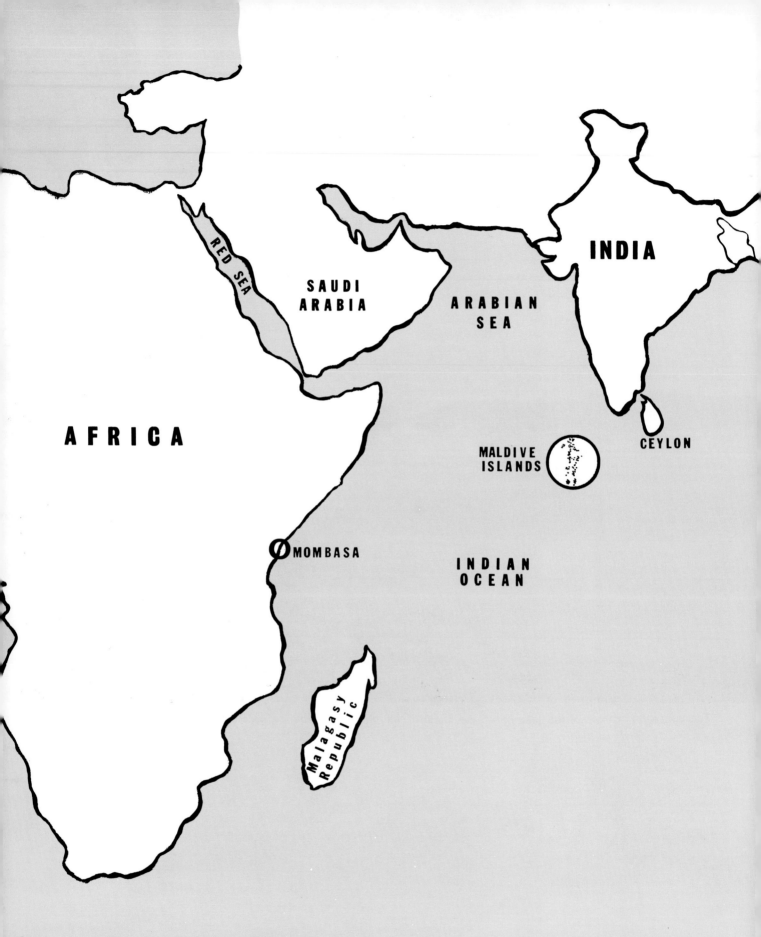

Family LABRIDAE

WRASSES

The wrasses were covered, at least partly, in Book 1 of this series. They are a large and varied group of fishes contained in approximately 50 to 60 genera. Estimates of the number of species in the family vary considerably, but usually exceed 500. Is it any wonder that a great deal of work has to be done on this group before some semblance of order can be gained?

The genus *Cheilinus* probably contains the largest species of wrasses in the Indo-Pacific region. *Cheilinus undulatus* individuals reaching a length of over seven feet and a weight of more than 200 pounds have been reported. The genus *Cheilinus* can be recognized by the following combination of characteristics: body fairly deep, compressed; scales relatively large, covering the head (except the snout) and the bases of the dorsal and anal fins (forming a sheath); snout large and lips thick; teeth uniserial, with a pair of enlarged canines in front of upper and lower jaws, those of lower jaw fitting between those of upper jaw when the mouth is closed; lateral line interrupted, one part running along the upper side below the dorsal fin, the other running along the center of the caudal peduncle; IX to X dorsal spines, 8 to 11 dorsal rays; anal fin with III spines and 8 or 9 rays. The caudal fin may be rounded, truncate, or have extensions forming a bi-lobed or tri-lobed fin. The color is usually greenish to brownish or red and usually there are reddish markings on the head especially around the eyes. Species of the genus *Cheilinus* can be identified to some extent by means of their color patterns. The accompanying photographs will serve to help in their recognition.

The genus *Coris* is well known to marine aquarists through the orange and white juvenile of *Coris gaimard*. In the Indian Ocean two similarly colored juveniles may be found, belonging to the species *Coris formosa* and *C. africana*.

3. *Cheilinus fasciatus* (Bloch). Banded *Cheilinus*. Maldives. Photo by Dr. Herbert R. Axelrod.

4. *Cheilinus fasciatus* (Bloch). The pattern of stripes and spots around the eyes helps to distinguish the species of this genus. Photo by Dr. Herbert R. Axelrod. Maldives.

5. *Cheilinus fasciatus* (Bloch). The enlarged canines of the lower jaw fit between those of the upper jaw when the mouth is closed. Photo by Dr. Herbert R. Axelrod. Maldives.

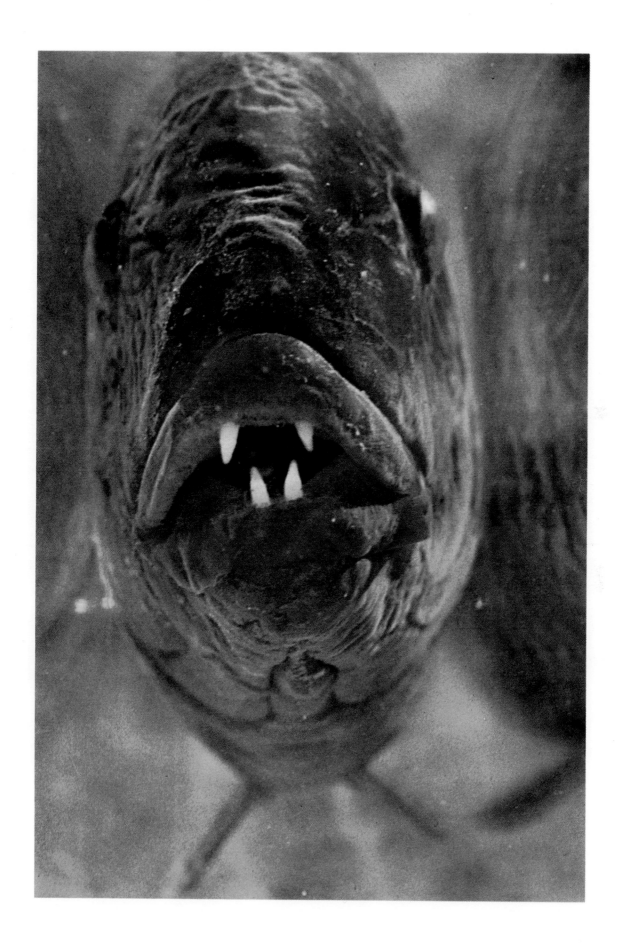

6. *Cheilinus trilobatus* Lacepede. Triple-tailed wrasse. This species exhibits a three-lobed caudal fin as an adult. Juvenile photographed by Ray Allard. Mombasa.

8. *Cheilinus bimaculatus* Cuvier & Valenciennes. The range of this species extends all the way to the Hawaiian Islands. Photo by Ray Allard. Mombasa.

9. *Cheilinus undulatus* Ruppell. This giant or humphead wrasse may grow as large as 7 feet. Photo by Ray Allard of a juvenile from Mombasa.

10. *Coris aygula* Lacepede. The two black and orange spots make this juvenile twinspot wrasse easily recognizable. Photo by Klaus Paysan.

11. *Coris aygula* Lacepede. The adult fish looks completely different from this attractive juvenile. Photo by Ray Allard. Mombasa.

12. *Coris gaimard* (Quoy & Gaimard). The clown wrasse still is colorful after changing from the juvenile to this subadult color pattern. This species apparently does not extend into the Indian Ocean, the reports being of a closely related species, *Coris africana.* Photo of a Philippine specimen by Dr. Herbert R. Axelrod.

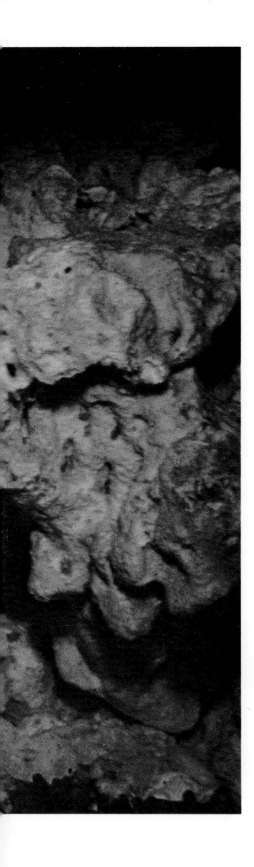

Basically the juveniles look very much alike in form and color pattern. *Coris formosa* can easily be recognized by the presence of an intense black spot in its dorsal fin. *Coris gaimard* is found in the Pacific Ocean and *C. africana* in the Indian Ocean, so no problem exists if the origin is known. The intermediate stages are similar as well but again have an easily recognizable distinguishing characteristic. The caudal fin of *Coris gaimard* at this stage is bright yellow, that of *Coris africana* is brownish with blue spots and that of *C. formosa* reddish with a wide clear or white edge. The distinctions can easily be seen by comparing the photos in this book with those on p. 140 (Book 1).

There are currently only two species recognized as belonging to the genus *Hemigymnus,* both appearing occasionally in aquarists' tanks. At very small sizes the relationship between these two species can be seen via the vertical banding. In *H. fasciatus* this banding remains as the fish grows (at least they are still visible in individuals up to 8 or 9 inches). In *H. melapterus* the banding fades quickly, except for the central band, which is widest, and the well known bicolored pattern becomes dominant. In larger fishes this bicolored pattern changes into a more uniform pattern.

The genus *Gomphosus* is characterized by the prolonged snout, as illustrated in the accompanying photos. The males and females can be distinguished easily by color pattern, the males being green and the females brown.

The genus *Bodianus* is one of the more difficult genera to work with systematically. The species of this genus, similar to some other genera of labrids, undergo a complete metamorphosis in color pattern, the young appearing completely different from the adults. In *Bodianus axillaris,* which is shown in the following pages, the prominent white spots will eventually disappear. The black spots, however, will remain, thus serving as distinguishing marks which identify

13. *Coris formosa* Bennett. The juvenile African clown wrasse looks very much like the juvenile *Coris gaimard* except for the black spot in its dorsal fin. Photo by W. Hoppe.

14. *Coris africana* Bennett. This African clown wrasse is in the midst of exchanging its juvenile livery for its adult colors. Photo by Ray Allard. Mombasa.

15. *Coris formosa* Bennett. The adult of this species looks very different from the adult *Coris africana* and *Coris gaimard*. Photo by Ray Allard. Mombasa.

16. *Coris caudimacula* Quoy & Gaimard. This young spottail wrasse differs from the larger one below, especially in the tail pattern. Photo by Ray Allard. Mombasa.

17. *Coris caudimacula* Quoy & Gaimard. At about 6 or 7 inches the spottail wrasse shows this pattern. Photo by Dr. Herbert R. Axelrod. Mombasa.

18. *Cirrhilabrus exquisitus* Smith. This very small individual (1 inch total length) was captured at the Maldive Islands, which may be the first record of its presence there. Photo by Dr. Herbert R. Axelrod.

19. *Cirrhilabrus exquisitus* Smith. The adult retains the black spot on the caudal peduncle. Photo by Ray Allard. Mombasa.

20. *Hemigymnus fasciatus* (Bloch). The intermediate stage of the banded wrasse. A 9-inch individual has less distinct bands. Photo by Dr. Herbert R. Axelrod.

21. *Hemigymnus fasciatus* (Bloch). This very young banded wrasse has not even developed the colorful head pattern of the subadult. Photo by Dr. Herbert R. Axelrod. Maldives.

22. *Hemigymnus melapterus*
(Bloch). The intermediate stage
of the half-and-half wrasse
retains the broad light band
which extends from the anterior
dorsal fin spines to the belly.
Photo by Dr. Herbert R. Axelrod.

23. *Hemigymnus melapterus* (Bloch). This rare photo of the very young stage of the half-and-half wrasse shows the broad light central band well developed. Photo by Ray Allard. Mombasa.

24. *Hemigymnus melapterus* (Bloch). The broad white band is starting to fade in this individual and will eventually disappear in the adult. Photo by Ray Allard. Mombasa.

25. *Gomphosus varius* Lacepede. The brown form of this species is the female. Photo by Ray Allard. Mombasa.

26. *Gomphosus varius* Lacepede. This extreme prolongation of the snout occurred in several families independently. Photo by Dr. Herbert R. Axelrod. Maldives.

27. *Gomphosus varius* Lacépede. The adult males of the bird wrasse are green. Photo by Dr. Herbert R. Axelrod.

28. *Gomphosus varius* Lacepede. This individual is slightly older than the one on the preceding page. Photo by Ray Allard. Mombasa.

the adult form (except perhaps *B. diana).* Other species of *Bodianus* have similar white markings but lack the black spots of *B. axillaris.* The genus itself can be characterized by a continuous lateral line, with 30 to 35 moderately large scales along it. The snout is pointed and the mouth large, containing a single series of teeth coalesced at their base. Two pairs of canines are present in each jaw, and a posterior canine is present. There are usually XII dorsal fin spines with some 8-10 rays.

The genus *Labrichthys* is related to the genus *Labroides* but is distinguished from it by having the body scales extending onto the dorsal and anal fins, the posterior edge of the preopercular bone not free, lips without lobes *(Labroides* has a forward projecting fleshy lobe at the corner of the lower lip), etc. The youngest form of *Labrichthys unilineata* shown here possesses a bluish-white lateral streak, from which its scientific name is apparently derived.

29. *Bodianus luteopunctatus* (Smith). The eyes of many fishes have anterior extensions to provide additional binocular vision. Photo by Dr. Herbert R. Axelrod. Maldives.

30. *Bodianus luteopunctatus* (Smith). In this individual much more yellow is present than on the one on the previous page. The band of red at the base of the pectoral fins is still prominent. Photo by Rodney Jonklaas. Ceylon.

31. *Bodianus luteopunctatus* (Smith). Little is known about this colourful wrasse. Photo by Dr. Herbert R. Axelrod. Maldives.

32. *Bodianus axillaris* Bennett. This juvenile is very different from the adult (see *Pacific Marine Fishes* Book 2). Photo by Dr. Herbert R. Axelrod. Maldives.

Bodianus axillaris Bennett. Coral hogfish. The three black spots distinguish this species. Photo by Roger Steene in Australia.

33. *Bodianus axillaris* Bennett. A larger specimen but still with the juvenile color pattern. Notice the resemblance between this juvenile and that of *Bodianus diana* p. 444, #310 (Book 2) below. Photo by Dr. Herbert R. Axelrod. Maldives.

Bodianus diana Coral hogfish. Photo by U. Erich Friese.

34. *Cheilio inermis* (Forskal). This is the chameleon of the wrasses, able to change from this green color to a brown depending upon its environment. Photo by Ray Allard. Mombasa.

35. *Hologymnosus semidiscus* (Lacepede). Another long and slender wrasse. This female striped cigar wrasse is colored differently from both the males and juveniles. Photo by Ray Allard. Mombasa.

36. *Labroides bicolor* Fowler & Bean. This is the intermediate stage in the changing of color patterns from juvenile to adult bicolor cleaner wrasse. Photo by Dr. Herbert R. Axelrod. Maldives.

37. *Labrichthys unilineata* Guichenot. The lateral stripe of the juvenile is fading appreciably though still visible. Photo by Ray Allard. Mombasa.

38. *Labrichthys unilineata* Guichenot. Here the lateral stripe of the juvenile is more pronounced. Photo by Dr. Herbert R. Axelrod. Maldives.

39. *Labrichthys unilineata* Guichenot. This fish is known for the peculiar pleated lips. Photo by Dr. Herbert R. Axelrod. Maldives.

40. *Stethojulis strigiventer* (Bennett). The female of this species (shown) is much less colorful than the male. Photo by Ray Allard. Mombasa.

41. *Stethojulis strigiventer* (Bennett). Against a green background this female appears greener than the one above. Photo by Ray Allard. Mombasa.

42. *Stethojulis strigiventer* (Bennett). This younger fish has dark spots at the base of the posterior rays of the dorsal and anal fins and lacks the cross-banding on the tail fin. Photo by Dr. Herbert R. Axelrod. Maldives.

Stethojulis has a continuous lateral line, a maxillary concealed by the preorbital, the head as well as the fins (except the base of the caudal fin) naked (without scales), the dorsal fin with IX spines and 10-14 rays and the anal fin with III spines (the first minute and partially embedded at the base of the second) and 10-12 rays.

Of the three species shown here the first two are represented by females of their respective species, and only *Stethojulis albovittata* by a male. The males of all three of these species exhibit similar longitudinal lines, the position and relative lengths of the markings serving to characterize the species.

The males of *Stethojulis strigiventer* (not shown) are green above, becoming yellow below the first blue line and eventually shading to white on the ventral surface. The uppermost blue line extends from the interorbital area through the eye and along the back (above the pectoral fin) to the base of the tail fin. A second blue line extends from the tip of the snout past the lower edge of the orbit to the upper edge of the pectoral fin base, and a third line extends from the edge of the gill cover past the lower edge of the pectoral base and ends on the side of the body at the level of the mid anal fin. A short blue streak extends backwards from the lower jaw. The white streaks in the females shown roughly correspond to the position of the lower two stripes of the male.

43. *Stethojulis axillaris* (Quoy & Gaimard). Although the color patterns of males and females are different they both have the bright orange patch above the pectoral fin as in this female. Photo by Ray Allard. Mombasa.

44. *Stethojulis albovittata* (Bonnaterre). The pattern of stripes on this male makes it readily identifiable. Photo by Dr. Herbert R. Axelrod. Mombasa.

45. *Halichoeres bimaculatus* Ruppell. This species apparently is found only in the Indian Ocean. Photo by Rodney Jonklaas. Ceylon.

46. *Halichoeres bimaculatus* Ruppell. The lateral blotch and the band along the sides are diagnostic. Photo by Dr. Herbert R. Axelrod. Maldives.

47. *Halichoeres nigrescens* (Schneider). Many species of the genus *Halichoeres* have a distinctive pattern of head stripes such as this one. Photo by Rodney Jonklaas. Ceylon.

The genus *Halichoeres* contains a rather large number of species which, unfortunately, are not well characterized. Males differ from females in color pattern, and juveniles may differ from them both. In addition there is a degree of variability wherein some individuals may possess certain spots and others may not. The color pattern remains, however, one of the best means of recognizing the species. The pattern of the head stripes, the stripes, arches or spots in the fins, lateral stripes, blotches or spots, and other features all contribute to species recognition. *Halichoeres centriquadratus* is one of the better known species of the genus and can easily be recognized by the checkerboard pattern of the body, (though other species exhibit such a pattern) and the yellow tail fin. The black spot at the base of the upper part of the tail fin may or may not be present. The juvenile of this species has a large black ocellated spot in the middle of the dorsal fin which the adults lack.

48. *Halichoeres melanochir* Fowler & Bean. The black band of the pectoral fin base and the dark spotting of the anterior back are diagnostic. Photo by Dr. Herbert R. Axelrod. Maldives.

49. *Halichoeres hoeveni* (Bleeker). This striped form has three ocellated spots (notice the little one in the first few spines of the dorsal fin). Photo by Dr. Herbert R. Axelrod. Maldives.

50. *Halichoeres notopsis* (Valenciennes). This striped species is easily distinguishable from the one above by color pattern. Photo by Dr. Herbert R. Axelrod. Maldives.

51a. *Halichoeres centriquadratus* (Lacepede).
Photo by Dr. Herbert R. Axelrod. Maldives.

51. *Halichoeres centriquadratus* (Lacepede). The checkerboard wrasse obviously deserves its common name as can be seen in this photograph. Photo by Dr. Herbert R. Axelrod. Maldives.

52. *Halichoeres centriquadratus* (Lacepede). The spot in the upper part of the caudal fin is quite distinct in this individual. Photo by Ray Allard. Mombasa.

53. *Halichoeres centriquadratus* (Lacepede). The young of this species looks quite different although the checkerboard pattern is becoming apparent. Photo by Ray Allard. Mombasa.

54. *Halichoeres centriquadratus* (Lacepede). Although this fish is almost identical to the one on the opposite page it comes from a different area of the Indian Ocean. Photo by Dr. Herbert R. Axelrod. Maldives.

55. *Halichoeres scapularis* (Bennett). The head pattern on this species is relatively simple. Photo by Dr. Herbert R. Axelrod. Maldives.

56. *Halichoeres scapularis* (Bennett). The dark lateral stripe gives this species its common name, zigzag wrasse. Photo by Ray Allard. Mombasa.

57. *Halichoeres scapularis* (Bennett). It is probable that this is the male of the species and the photo above is of the female. Photo by Dr. Herbert R. Axelrod. Maldives.

58. *Halichoeres kawarin* Bleeker. This species is generally found in weedy areas. Photo by Ray Allard. Mombasa.

59. *Halichoeres kawarin* Bleeker. The range of this species is large, but it apparently is not very common throughout its range. Photo by Ray Allard. Mombasa.

60. *Thalassoma amblycephalus* (Bleeker). This is a juvenile paddlefin or rainbow wrasse, quite different from the adult below. Photo by Dr. John E. Randall.

61. *Thalassoma amblycephalus* (Bleeker). This adult male clearly shows the black mark on the pectoral fin from which the common name paddlefin wrasse originated. Photo by Dr. Herbert R. Axelrod. Maldives.

62. *Thalassoma hebraicum* (Lacepede). This is a typical individual of this species with the yellow anterior band. Photo by Ray Allard. Mombasa.

63. *Thalassoma hebraicum* (Lacepede). This specimen lacking the yellow band might be a female. Photo by Dr. Herbert R. Axelrod. Mombasa.

64. A tiny wrasse (less than one inch total length). It is probably the young of *Thalassoma amblycephalus* (Bleeker). Photo by Dr. Herbert R. Axelrod. Maldives.

65. *Thalassoma lunare* (Linnaeus). In this lighter colored individual the dorsal and caudal spots are very noticeable. Photo by Ray Allard. Mombasa.

66. *Thalassoma lunare* (Linnaeus). A more typical specimen with the dorsal fin spot faded. Photo by Dr. Herbert R. Axelrod. Mombasa.

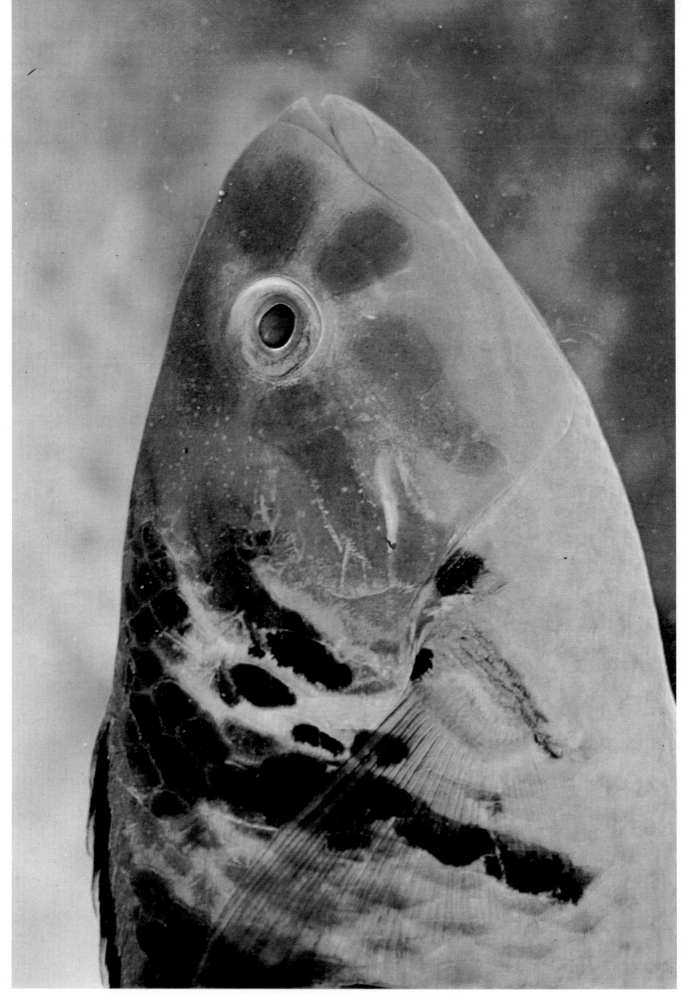

68. *Thalassoma hardwicke* (Bennett). In this individual the pink lateral stripe is evident, as is the blackish spot in the anal fin. Photo by Dr. Herbert R. Axelrod. Maldives.

67. *Thalassoma hardwicke* (Bennett). It is always a source of wonder how such intricate patterns evolve in some of the wrasses. Photo by Dr. Herbert R. Axelrod. Maldives.

The genus *Thalassoma* has an elongate body which is slightly compressed. The lateral line is usually complete but takes a sharp downward turn below the soft dorsal fin. The teeth are similar to those of other genera of wrasses which have an enlarged pair of canines in the end of the lower jaw which fit between a similarly enlarged pair in the upper jaw. The species do not grow overly large, most being between 7 and 10 inches in length. Juveniles are characteristically different from the adults, and there is a supermale form present. The pattern of the pectoral fin is important in recognizing species, there being a blackish marking especially noticeable in living fishes, since the pectoral fins are the main source of propulsion in this group. The dorsal fin is usually composed of VIII spines and 13 rays and the anal fin III spines and 11 rays. The scales are relatively large, less than 30 in the lateral line.

69. *Thalassoma hardwicke* (Bennett). The black banding has become partially obscured by the reddish-pink color. Photo by Dr. Herbert R. Axelrod. Maldives.

70. *Thalassoma hardwicke* (Bennett). This young specimen, probably a female, lacks the anal fin spot but possesses a dark spot in the central part of the dorsal fin. Photo by Ray Allard. Mombasa.

71. *Thalassoma quinquevittata* (Lay & Bennett). The pinkish-red "ladder" pattern is common to several different species of *Thalassoma*. Photo by Dr. Herbert R. Axelrod. Maldives.

72 and 73. *Thalassoma umbrostigma* (Ruppell) (above and below). It is quite possible that this species is merely a synonym of *T. purpureum* (Forskal). Upper photo by Rodney Jonklaas, Ceylon; lower photo by Ray Allard, Mombasa.

74 and 75. *Thalassoma janseni* (Bleeker). (above and below). The extent of the dark bars is variable, allowing differing amounts of the yellow ground color to show. Photo above by Rodney Jonklaas, Ceylon; photo below by Dr. Herbert R. Axelrod, Maldives.

76. *Anampses caeruleopunctatus* Ruppell. The spots on the head of this juvenile specimen are beginning to coalesce into lines. Photo by Ray Allard. Mombasa.

77. *Anampses caeruleopunctatus* Ruppell. A smaller individual with spots separate and a broader white edge to the tail fin. Compare this juvenile with the adult (*Pacific Marine Fishes* Book 2, p. 440 #299). Photo by Ray Allard. Mombasa.

78. *Macropharyngodon varialvus* Smith. It is not yet known what changes, if any, this species might undergo with growth. Photo by Ray Allard. Mombasa.

79. This young *Pseudocheilinus* has not developed the pattern by which it can be recognized. Photo by Dr. Herbert R. Axelrod. Maldives.

80. *Pseudocheilinus hexataenia* (Bleeker). This beautiful species does not grow to more than 4 inches. Photo by Dr. Herbert R. Axelrod. Maldives.

Family SCARIDAE

PARROTFISHES

The Parrotfishes have been divided into two subfamilies, the Scarinae and the Sparisomatinae. These subfamilies are very close and it would be almost impossible to decide to which subfamily a species belongs simply by gross observation. The Scarinae have 2-4 rows of cheek scales (below the eye) although the second row may be represented by a single scale, whereas in the Sparisomatinae there is a single row usually composed of 2 to 5 scales. A second somewhat easily used character to separate the two subfamilies is that the teeth (plate) of the upper jaw are included within that of the lower jaw in the Sparisomatinae; in the Scarinae the edge of the plate of the lower jaw fits within that of the upper jaw when the mouth is closed.

In most texts the brightly colored adult male parrotfishes and occasionally a female are illustrated. Young fishes are mostly ignored for the simple reason that determination of the species is extremely difficult if not impossible at the present state of knowledge on these fishes. In many cases even the adults cannot easily be identified with existing literature. The color patterns are very important in species recognition and living specimens may be needed to finally resolve many of the problems besetting this family. The diagnostic colors fade very quickly after the fishes die, giving ichthyologists additional causes for confusion.

81. Young parrotfish, *Scarus sexvittatus* Ruppell. Photo by Ray Allard. Mombasa.

82. This juvenile parrotfish may turn out to be *Scarus lepidus* Jenyns. Photo by Ray Allard. Mombasa.

83. Red fins and bluish or greenish body is characteristic for the male *Scarus sexvittatus* Ruppell. Photo by Dr. Herbert R. Axelrod. Mombasa.

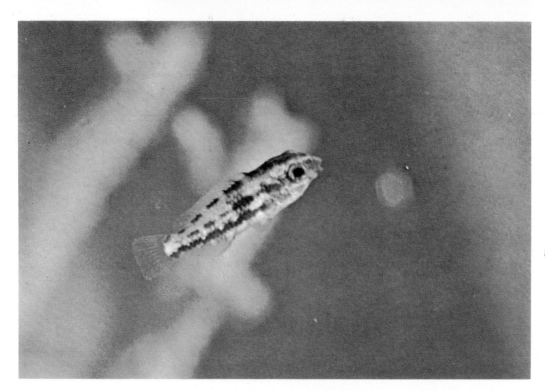

84. A tiny fish that is barely recognizable as a parrotfish. Photo by Dr. Herbert R. Axelrod. Maldives.

85. *Leptoscarus vaigiensis* (Quoy & Gaimard). This species extends from the central Pacific Ocean all the way to the Mediterranean Sea. Photo by Dr. Herbert R. Axelrod. Maldives.

86. The bright red of the anterior ventral area including the head is found in *Scarus madagascariensis* (Steindachner). The other fish with red fins in this photo is a snapper (*Lutjanus*). Photo by Dr. Herbert R. Axelrod. Maldives.

87. Young parrotfish. The spots resemble somewhat those of *Scarus chlorodon* Jenyns. That species has been known as *Callyodon improvisus* Smith in the Western Indian Ocean. Photo by Ray Allard. Mombasa.

88. Probably the most common juvenile color pattern is the mottled brownish or greenish of this individual. Photo by Ray Allard. Mombasa. Possibly *Calotomus spinidens* (Quoy & Gaimard).

89. *Scarus* sp. This striking color pattern will probably disappear with age, being replaced by one totally different. Photo by Dr. Herbert R. Axelrod. Maldives.

90. *Gobiodon citrinus* (Ruppell). This small goby has a very compressed body. Photo by Ray Allard. Mombasa.

91. *Eleotroides strigatus* (Broussonet). The golden headed goby reaches a length of about 5 inches. Photo by Dr. Herbert R. Axelrod. Maldives.

Family GOBIIDAE

GOBIES AND SLEEPERS

Gobies and sleepers were (and still are) often placed in separate families, Gobiidae and Eleotridae. The basic character used to distinguish these fishes was the presence of a membrane uniting the pelvic fins (in the gobies) which was absent in the sleepers. Those fishes with the pelvic fins united to form a sucking disc were placed in the Gobiidae and those with separate pelvic fins were placed in the Eleotridae. However, certain intermediate genera were discovered wherein the uniting membrane was reduced, and those genera could not be placed in either family with certainty. It was decided that this distinction was not enough to warrant retention of two separate families. Other more substantial characters may be found which will place the separation on a firmer footing. There are other families of goby-like fishes included in the suborder Gobioidei (ex. Kraemeriidae, Microdesmidae, etc.), but they do not concern us at this time.

Of the fishes represented on the adjacent pages only *Eleotroides* is a sleeper, the others being representatives of various goby genera. The distinctions of the pelvic fins can be seen in these photos. Those of fig. #92 are obviously separate, whereas those of fig. #96 are united to form the tell-tale disc.

Eleotroides strigatus is usually found in tropical waters around areas associated with reefs. They may utilize the dead coral or part of a rock as part of their burrow. The white coloring of the body blends in with the white of the sand or dead coral, making them difficult to spot (except for the blue and yellow markings of the head).

92. *Eleotroides strigatus* (Broussonet). The pattern of blue markings on the head and body is almost identical with that on specimens from the Pacific. Photo by Dr. Herbert R. Axelrod. Maldives.

93. Unidentified
sleeper
(eleotrid).
Photo by
Dr. Herbert
R. Axelrod.
Maldives.

94. *Amblygobius albimaculatus* (Ruppell). The dark phase shows off some markings not evident in the lighter colored fish. Photo by Dr. Herbert R. Axelrod. Maldives.

95. *Acentrogobius cauerensis* (Bleeker). The pattern of dashes in the dorsal fin aids in the identification of this species. Photo by Ray Allard. Mombasa .

96. *Amblygobius albimaculatus* (Ruppell). The pelvic disc is well discernible in this photograph. Photo by Ray Allard. Mombasa.

Family BLENNIIDAE
BLENNIES

Blennies have been covered to some extent on pages 159-160. As noted they differ from another large family of blenny-like fishes (Clinidae) by lacking scales. They differ from the Blennioid family Trypterygiidae also by the absence of scales. The Trypterygiidae differ from the Clinidae by possessing three dorsal fins and scales of moderate size, whereas the clinids have only two dorsal fins and small scales that are imbedded in the skin.

The different genera of blennies are recognized by a variety of characteristics. The cirri, tentacles, and other projections on the head are helpful in this distinction. In *Exallias* and *Cirripectes* there is a row of cirri crossing the neck (usually numbering between 25-45). These are noticeable in the photos of *Cirripectes variolosus* and *Exallias brevis* presented in these pages. *Exallias* is distinguished from *Cirripectes* by possessing a pair of short tentacles on either side of the chin. On the other hand *Salarias* and *Ecsenius* have but a single or branched tentacle on either side of the neck. Other blennies may have a single unbranched tentacle located above the eye, such as in *Istiblennius* (which also lacks the neck tentacles), or a single many-branched tentacle over the eye, such as in *Entamacrodus*. In some genera there may be a fleshy crest on the head, but this cannot be used as a generic character since the crest may be present in the male but absent in the females of certain species. This is the case in various species of genus *Petroscirtes*, (which incidentally also has a well developed branched supraorbital tentacle). *Petroscirtes*, however, has the gill opening reduced to a small hole above the base of the pectoral fin.

97. *Plagiotremus* sp. This recently discovered species is in the process of being scientifically described. Photo by Dr. Herbert R. Axelrod. Maldives.

98. *Cirripectes variolosus* (Cuvier & Valenciennes). This species is found in both the Indian and Pacific Oceans. Photo by Ray Allard. Mombasa.

99. *Meiacanthus mossambicus* Smith. Species like this one spend some of their time in midwater in contrast to strictly bottom type blennies. Photo by Ray Allard. Mombasa.

100. *Haliophis guttatus* (Forskal). Family Congrogadidae. Photo by Ray Allard. Mombasa.

101. *Salarius fasciatus* (Bloch). The cirri on the head are found in many blennies and are used for identification purposes. Photo by Ray Allard. Mombasa.

102. *Petroscirtes mitratus* Ruppell. The extended anterior dorsal fin spines are characteristic of the genus. Photo by Ray Allard. Mombasa.

103. *Exallias brevis* (Kner). This blenny has well developed cirri on the head. Photo by Ray Allard. Mombasa.

104. *Exallias brevis* (Kner). Notice the differentiated lower pectoral rays. Photo by Ray Allard. Mombasa.

Family CARACANTHIDAE
VELVETFISHES

Caracanthids are strange little fishes that have puzzled scientists for quite some time. They have been moved around from one group to another, never really fitting comfortably into any of them. The recent consensus, however, places the caracanthids in the order Scorpaeniformes and suborder Scorpaenoidei along with fishes like the turkeyfishes, stonefishes, sea robins, etc.

The velvetfishes are small in size, often not exceeding the size of a silver dollar. They are laterally compressed, deep-bodied, and generally orbicular or suborbicular in body shape. Although their heads are not so covered with spines as most other members of the suborder, they do have spines on the preoperculum and interoperculum, a row of tubercles from the interorbital to the occiput, a nasal spine, and a strong preorbital spine that is extensible outward. The single dorsal fin is moderately notched. The pelvic fins, although present, are greatly reduced and inconspicuous.

The common name velvetfishes comes from the appearance of the body and head, which are covered with small, close-set dermal papillae. If ever there was such a thing as a furry fish, this one would probably come closest, at least in appearance.

These fishes are often seen hiding among the branches of corals, especially genus *Poecilopora,* where they remain protected. One of the authors (WEB) has captured caracanthids in Hawaii by lifting the coral head out of the water and shaking the fish out into a net. Often they will remain wedged in the coral and additional effort must be expended to extract them.

105. *Caracanthus maculatus* (Gray). The pelvic fins are almost obsolete in the velvetfishes. Photo by Ray Allard. Mombasa.

106. The striped fish in the center is *Cephalopholis argus*. To its left is a butterflyfish (*Forcipiger*), and to the far left is a species of *Monotaxis*. Photo by Dr. Herbert R. Axelrod. Maldives.

Family SERRANIDAE

GROUPERS

The identification of groupers is very difficult. Aside from the usual problems with variable color patterns, distinctions are often based upon the presence or absence of canine teeth. The differences between species and even genara are very small. *Cephalopholis* for instance has canine teeth and teeth on the palate as do *Variola, Epinephelus,* and *Plectropomus. Cromileptes* has no canine teeth, although the palate is toothed. *Variola* and *Cephalopholis* differ in that one (*Variola*) has curved canines on each side of the jaw (in addition to those in front) which are lacking in the other *(Cephalopholis).* Both of these genera have nine dorsal fin spines and 13-14 rays in comparison to *Epinephelus,* which has eleven dorsal fin spines (although nine or ten may be possible but rare) and 14-18 rays. *Anyperodon* lacks teeth on the palate and has eleven dorsal fin spines as well as 14-15 rays.

The above genera, along with others, are placed in the subfamily Epinephelinae. This subfamily is characterized by having a moderately compressed oblong body, a slightly protractile large mouth, and small to moderate adherent scales sometimes embedded in the skin. The slightly arched lateral line is complete; the dorsal fin is entire or slightly notched between the soft and spinous parts; jaws, vomer and palatines have bands of small conical teeth, those in inner series of jaws often depressible; those in outer may in part be composed of enlarged canines.

The subfamily Grammistinae has a single dorsal fin, but the spiny and soft sections are separated by a deep notch; the preopercle and opercle have prominent spines; the anal fin has up to 3 spines; and there are bands of villiform teeth on the vomer and palatines as well as in the jaws.

The Anthiinae (*Anthias, Mirolabrichthys, etc.*) were covered on page 489.

107. *Epinephelus fasciatus* (**Forskal**). This grouper grows to about 18 inches in length. Photo by Ray Allard. Mombasa.

108. *Cephalopholis boenack* (Bloch). At times the blue lines of this fish are much more noticeable and serve as an aid to identification. Photo by Dr. Herbert R. Axelrod. Maldives.

109. *Epinephelus fario* (Thunberg). This young spotted grouper will eventually reach a full size of about two feet. Photo by Ray Allard. Mombasa.

110. *Epinephelus merra* Bloch. Groupers such as this species are among the larger predators of the reef. Photo by Dr. Herbert R. Axelrod. Maldives.

111. *Cephalopholis rogaa* (Forskal) with the triggerfish *Balistapus undulatus* (Mungo Park). The orange fish are *Anthias* sp. Photo by Dr. Herbert R. Axelrod. Maldives.

112. *Anyperodon leucogrammicus* (Cuvier & Valenciennes). The red color of the spotting of this fish is lost in the deeper water where everything appears blue. Photo by Dr. Herbert R. Axelrod. Maldives.

113. *Mirolabrichthys evansi* (Smith). This species was recently switched from genus *Anthias* to *Miro-labrichthys* because of the development of the snout. Photo by Ray Allard. Mombasa.

114. *Mirolabrichthys evansi* (Smith). Apparently this is the young of the above species. The stripe through the eye is just developing. Photo by Dr. Herbert R. Axelrod. Maldives.

115. *Anthias squamipinnis* (Peters). This species is probably the most well known of the anthiids. The male is shown here. Photo by Dr. Herbert R. Axelrod. Maldives.

116. *Mirolabrichthys evansi* (Smith). A school of these fishes hovering around some coconut palm trunks. Photo by Dr. Herbert R. Axelrod. Maldives.

117. *Mirolabrichthys evansi* (Smith). A cleaner wrasse, *Labroides dimidiatus* is giving this individual the once over. Photo by Dr. Herbert R. Axelrod. Maldives.

118. *Cephalopholis leopardus* (Lacepede). This beautiful grouper can grow to a size of over 16 inches. Photo by Dr. Herbert R. Axelrod. Maldives.

119. *Grammistes sexlineatus* (Thunberg). The golden-striped grouper does very well in marine aquaria, especially if fed on small fishes. Photo by Ray Allard. Mombasa.

Family SCORPAENIDAE
SCORPIONFISHES

Scorpionfishes have two major features which are used for purposes of identification, (1) the structure of the head and (2) of the pectoral fins. The head is large and usually exhibits several ridges and/or spines, along with various tentacles and skin flaps. In addition, there are depressions or pits which are useful in recognizing the genera of scorpionfishes. The pectoral fins are large, in some forms such as *Pterois* and *Dendrochirus* extremely large, with branched and unbranched rays as well as separation of major importance.

In the genus *Pterois* (lionfishes, turkeyfish, etc.) all of the pectoral rays are elongate, unbranched, and the upper rays are free from one another, at least for the most part, the membrane connecting them extending only partway from the base of the fin. The closely related genus *Dendrochirus* also has elongated pectoral fins, but some of the upper middle rays are branched and none of the rays are free from the membrane as in the genus *Pterois*. The contrast between the two types of pectoral fins can be seen in the accompanying photos.

Of the genera with less spectacular pectoral fin development most also have 12 or 13 dorsal fin spines. *Scorpionopsis* and *Sebastapistes* have 12 dorsal spines but *Scorpionopsis* lacks palatine teeth which are present in *Sebastapistes*. *Parascorpaena* also has 12 dorsal spines and palatine teeth but has mostly cycloid scales, 40 or more in a longitudinal series above the lateral line, whereas *Sebastapistes* has mostly ctenoid scales, usually between 35-40 in a longitudinal series above the lateral line.

Scorpaenodes is among the genera with a normal complement of 13 dorsal fin spines as well as a toothless palate.

120. *Dendrochirus brachypterus* (Cuvier & Valenciennes). This species resembles, but is not, a member of the true lionfishes or turkeyfishes (*Pterois*). Photo by Ray Allard. Mombasa.

121.   *Parascorpaena aurita* (Ruppell). The head, except for the spination, resembles that of some of the blennies with all the fringes and tentacles. Photo by Ray Allard. Mombasa.

122. *Sebastapistes oglinus* Smith(?). The blotchy appearance of many scorpionfishes make them difficult to see in their natural environment. Photo by Dr. Herbert R. Axelrod. Maldives.

123. *Scorpaenopsis cirrhosus* (Thunberg). Scorpionfishes will eat both fishes and invertebrates and are usually easy to maintain in an aquarium. Photo by Dr. Herbert R. Axelrod. Maldives.

124. *Sebastapistes kowiensis* Smith. The large pectoral fin with its fleshy rays is clearly visible. Photo by Ray Allard. Mombasa.

125. *Scorpaenopsis gibbosa* (Bloch). This fish is sometimes confused with the more dangerous stonefish (*Synanceja*). Photo by Ray Allard. Mombasa.

126. *Pterois antennata* Bloch. Turkeyfishes are often found in caves upside down like these two. Photo by Dr. Herbert R. Axelrod. Maldives.

127. *Pterois antennata* Bloch. The conspicuous
coloration and finnage of the turkeyfishes
may serve warning to potential attackers.
Photo by Dr. Herbert R. Axelrod. Maldives.

128. *Dendrochirus zebra* (Cuvier & Valenciennes). This genus is very much like *Pterois* in color and
appearance but differs in pectoral fin structure among other things. Photo by Dr. Herbert R. Axelrod.
Maldives.

Family CIRRHITIDAE
HAWKFISHES

The hawkfishes are a small family of fishes comprising only about three dozen species. Most of them, in fact all but two or three species, occur in our area of coverage, the Indo-Pacific. The others are found in the Atlantic Ocean.

The genera aquarists are most apt to become acquainted with are *Oxycirrhites, Paracirrhites, Amblycirrhitus,* and *Cirrhitichthys.* The genera are difficult to distinguish, as the differences are slight or obscure, and the aquarist must usually work with live fishes that cannot be placed under a microscope for closer examination. Most of these cirrhitids have ten dorsal fin spines and ten to thirteen dorsal fin rays. Other genera, such as *Isobuna* and *Serranocirrhi-*

tus, have more rays, the latter genus with about 19. *Oxycirrhites* has a sharply pointed snout (as mentioned previously), rather elongate in the case of *O. typus,* 13 dorsal rays, cirri on the membranes behind the spine tips, giving them a tufted appearance, and about three rows of enlarged scales on the cheek. The other genera have more normal snouts. In *Amblycirrhitus* the first two pectoral rays are simple and unbranched, whereas *Paracirrhites* and *Cirrhitichthys* have the first pectoral ray simple and followed by the branched rays. *Paracirrhites* usually has 11 dorsal fin rays, 5 to 6 rows of enlarged scales on the cheek, and no incision on the front of upper or lower lips. *Cirrhitichthys* normally has 12 dorsal fin rays, only 4 rows of enlarged cheek scales, incisions on both upper and lower lips (especially lower), and a tufted appearance of the dorsal fin spine membranes like

129. *Paracirrhites arcatus* (Cuvier & Valenciennes). The Pacific form is virtually identical to this one (see Book 1 photo 272). Photo by Dr. Herbert R. Axelrod. Mombasa.

130. *Paracirrhites arcatus* (Cuvier & Valenciennes). Coral heads are typical resting places for these hawkfishes. The fishes on the left belong to the genus *Dascyllus.* Photo by Dr. Herbert R. Axelrod. Maldives.

131. *Monotaxis grandoculis* (Forskäl). The younger fishes in this species have characteristic vertical white lines crossing the body. The one on the head is last to fade. Photo by Dr. Herbert R. Axelrod. Maldives.

that of *Oxycirrhites*. These distinctions only work when comparing the genera mentioned; the lesser known genera (at least to aquarists) like *Hughichthys, Cyprinocirrhites, Cirrhitops*, etc., need additional clarification which will not be discussed at this time.

They make excellent aquarium fishes when kept with tankmates too large to swallow.

Family LETHRINIDAE
EMPEROR BREAM

The lethrinids are moderate-size perch-like fishes occurring almost exclusively in tropical waters. They are found around coral reefs in coastal waters where they are sought after for food. The flesh of lethrinids is reported to be very good and members of the family have become commercially valuable as food fishes. They can be captured by means of hand lines or traps.

Emperor bream have a deep pointed head which is scaleless, along with the cheeks. The operculum, however, is scaly. The preorbital is broad and its edge largely overlaps the maxilla. The dorsal fin is continuous and the lateral line complete; the mouth, which is provided with thickened, fleshy lips, is of moderate size and slightly

132. *Monotaxis grandoculis* (Forskal). The specific name of this fish refers to its very large eyes. Photo by Dr. Herbert R. Axelrod. Maldives.

protractile. There are almost always ten dorsal fin spines and nine rays, and three anal fin spines with eight rays. There are few (around 5 to 6) short gill rakers.

These fishes are reported to be very difficult to identify. Museum specimens lose most of their colors very quickly, whereas those observed on the reefs have involved patterns of bars, blotches, reticulations, etc., which give them all a sameness of appearance. According to Dr. J.L.B. Smith

133. *Lethrinus* sp. Juvenile, 4.25 inches standard length. Photo by Ray Allard. Mombasa.

(1959), the best time to identify these fishes is straight from the water after the darker markings, bars, etc., have faded and before the colorful patterns underlying them fade as well. He compares the difficulty in working with this group to that of working with the parrotfishes, notorious for their problems.

In the most recent classification the genus *Monotaxis,* often placed in its own family, is included in the family Lethrinidae. It is treated as such here.

134. *Monotaxis grandoculis* (Forskal). Maldives.

The parrotfish in the corner is probably a male *Scarus frenatus*. Photo by Dr. Herbert R. Axelrod.

Family NEMIPTERIDAE
BUTTERFLY-BREAM

The composition of this and other closely related families is very unstable. Genera are constantly being switched from one family to another and almost every genus in this group seems to have been raised to family level at one time or another. Close examination is therefore necessary to distinguish the families, they are so much alike. Included in this tight-knit area are the Nemipteridae, Lethrinidae, Pentapodidae, Pomadasyidae, etc.

The nemipterids are perch-like but with a slightly elongate body. The ctenoid scales are moderate or small, absent on parts of the head (snout and jaws, preorbital, suborbital) but present on the preopercle and opercle. The single dorsal fin normally has ten spines (as in the lethrinids) and nine to ten rays. The caudal fin is forked or at least emarginate.

Although one of the genera now included in the Nemipteridae, *Scolopsis*, once was placed in a family by itself on the basis of a sharp spine below the eye, this difference is not considered great enough to warrant such an action. The differences between other genera are often slight, such as *Gnathodentex* being separable by the upper border of the maxilla possessing a strongly denticulate ridge from *Nemipterus*.

The butterfly-bream are marine fishes of the Indo-Pacific region, usually encountered around coral reefs. They are carnivores with anterior teeth being canines or incisors.

Many of these fishes, especially those of the genus *Nemipterus*, are brightly colored and have filaments trailing from their caudal fins.

The closely related grunts and sweet lips, family Pomadasyidae, have been covered in Book 1, p. 222. Additional photos of these fishes follow the nemipterid genus *Scolopsis*.

135. *Gnathodentex aurolineatus* (Lacepede). The yellow stripes and bright spot below the soft dorsal fin are much faded in this individual. Photo by Dr. Herbert R. Axelrod. Maldives.

136. *Gnathodentex aurolineatus* (Lacepede). A small school of the spot bream with the yellow colors and white spot prominent. Photo by Rodney Jonklaas. Ceylon.

137. *Scolopsis ghanam* (Forskal). The pattern of pale lines distinguishes this species from others in the genus. Photo by Ray Allard. Mombasa.

138. *Scolopsis bilineatus* (Bloch). This is probably the best known scolopsid to the aquarist. Photo by Dr. Herbert R. Axelrod. Maldives.

139. *Gaterin orientalis* (Bloch). The adult shown here is quite different from its juvenile (see p. 347). Photo by Rodney Jonklaas. Ceylon.

140. *Gaterin gaterinus* (Forskal). This juvenile is only about 4 inches long. As an adult it will be spotted, not striped. Photo by Ray Allard. Mombasa.

141. *Gaterin punctatissimus* (Playfair). The heavy built lips of these fishes probably led to the common name sweetlips. Photo of an adult by Rodney Jonklaas. Ceylon.

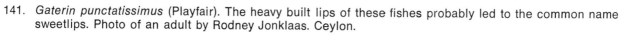

142. *Gaterin orientalis* (Bloch). The underwater flash highlights this individual sweetlips in a typical coral setting. Photo by Dr. Herbert R. Axelrod. Maldives.

143. This young *Lutjanus* (2 inches SL) appears to be closely related to *L. sanguineus* (Cuvier & Valenciennes) and *L. gibbus* (Forskal) or could be the juvenile of one of them. Photo by Ray Allard. Mombasa.

144. *Lutjanus bohar* (Forskal). The two pearly spots on the back help identify this species. Photo by Ray Allard. Mombasa.

Family LUTJANIDAE
SNAPPERS

The snappers were covered in part in Book 1, p. 221. This family is a mixture of fish types, as can be seen in the photographic coverage in this set of books.

Macolor niger is unusual in that the juvenile is distinctively patterned in black and white. At this point it is a very attractive fish for a marine aquarium. As it grows, however, the white spotting gradually disappears. The adult is a more sombre-colored fish. The gill rakers are numerous, 40 + 75 on the first arch, long and slender. There are narrow bands of small teeth in the jaws with the typical few enlarged canines in the anterior part of the upper jaw. Vomerine teeth are present in a "V" shape. It reaches a length of about 2 feet.

Lutjanus sebae is a very popular aquarium fish. The color pattern is distinctive, and specific characteristics need not be added here. This fish can readily be identified by reference to the photo on the following page. It soon outgrows its aquarium, as its full size is reached at a length of over three feet and a weight of almost 50 pounds.

The species of *Caesio* are known under the common name of fusilier or, in some cases, bananafish. These are small- to moderate-size fishes usually about a foot in length at maturity. They are distinguished from the bulk of the snappers by their general body shape and the presence of a bony projection on the intermaxilla. They occur

145. *Lutjanus johni* (Bloch). Perhaps the most typical shape of a snapper in shown by this individual. Many species also have the large black spot on or near the lateral line as in this one. Photo by Ray Allard. Mombasa.

146. *Lutjanus sebae* (Cuvier). Young emperor snappers are well known to marine aquarists. This species extends from Africa to the Pacific Ocean. Photo by D. Terver of the Nancy Aquarium, France.

147. *Macolor niger* (Forskal). At 2-3" this species is strikingly patterned. By 12" much of the white is lost. Photo by Dr. Herbert R. Axelrod. Maldives.

in schools, as can be seen in several of the underwater photos in this book, around reefs and rocky areas. The dorsal and anal fin spines are weak and slender. The basic colors are blue, yellow, white and red. They are able to change from blue and white to blue and red within a very short time. Our photos show more or less intermediate stages in this changeover.

The fusiliers are very abundant in the Indian Ocean and add a great deal of color to the reefs as they swim in synchronized schools in their search for food. It is doubtful whether these fusiliers would survive for any length of time in an aquarium.

The species of the genus *Aphareus* are called jobfishes or small-toothed jobfishes. Unlike many of the other snapper genera,

the jobfishes have a toothless palate. The cheeks and operculum are scaly, but the preorbital and preopercular flange are scaleless. This latter characteristic can be seen in the photo of *Aphareus furcatus*. The last rays of the dorsal and anal fin are prolonged into filaments; as the fish grows older a second point is produced on the pectoral fin by the prolongation of the lower rays. The shape of the body, the strong caudal peduncle and the forked tail fin seem to indicate this type fish is a powerful swimmer. The mouth is large but the teeth are small, arranged in several rows in the front of the jaws and a single row on the side. The typical enlarged canines are not present in this group.

148. *Aphareus furcatus* (Lacepede). This snapper apparently is from deeper waters. No account of the color of this species mentions the blue shown in the photo although *A. flavivultus,* a supposed synonym, was described as "dirty violet." Photo by Dr. Herbert R. Axelrod. Maldives.

149. *Caesio xanthonotus* (Bleeker). This and other species of *Caesio* are often found in the stomachs of tunas. Photo by Ray Allard. Mombasa.

150. *Pterocaesio tile* (Cuvier & Valenciennes). The dark bars in the tail fin aid in the identification of this species. Photo by Dr. Herbert R. Axelrod. Maldives.

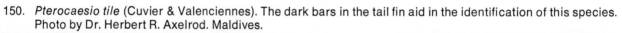

151. *Caesio caerulaureus* (Lacepede). Although this fish looks very much like the one opposite, it is placed in a separate genus. Photo by Ray Allard. Mombasa.

Family APOGONIDAE
CARDINALFISHES

To identify a cardinalfish, that is to recognize a fish as belonging to the cardinalfish family, is relatively easy. Most cardinalfishes have a basic similar appearance with the exception of course of the color pattern. But problems begin when one tries to differentiate the different cardinalfish genera.

The genus *Apogon* contains more species than any other genus in the family. The number of species included is quite variable depending upon whether the taxonomist treating the family is a "splitter," dividing the genus up into smaller genera, or a "lumper," who considers the differences found not significant enough to warrant this breakdown. Some "genera" used in this book would not be used by a lumper (ex. *Apogonichthyoides, Fowleria*) but are given here to indicate some of the different categories used in these separations. *Archamia* is usually regarded as a separate genus easily distinguishable by having a greater number of anal fin rays (12-18) than does genus *Apogon* (8-13).

One of the differences that helps break the family down into more manageable units is the presence or absence of enlarged canine teeth in the jaws. *Cheilodipterus* is one genus which possesses these teeth, which are clearly visible in the photographs on the following pages. With the exception of these teeth the species look very much like species of *Apogon* or other cardinalfishes. *Synagrops* also is characterized by having enlarged canine teeth but these spe-

152. *Apogon savayensis* (Gunther). The width of the dark triangle below the eye is important; compare it with the fish in the photo opposite. Photo by Dr. Herbert R. Axelrod. Maldives.

153. *Apogon cyanosoma* (Bleeker). This colorful little cardinalfish would make a very nice addition to an aquarium. Photo by Ray Allard. Mombasa.

154. *Apogon nubilis* (Garman). In a certain light the body exhibits purplish reflections, making this a very attractive fish. Photo by Dr. Herbert R. Axelrod. Maldives.

155. *Cheilodipterus lineatus* (Linnaeus). When adding this species to an aquarium, make sure the other fish can defend themselves against its mouthful of teeth. Photo by Dr. Herbert R. Axelrod. Maldives.

156. *Cheilodipterus lineatus* (Linnaeus). The close-up on the opposite page is of the head of this fish. The teeth are still visible in this photo. Photo by Dr. Herbert R. Axelrod. Maldives.

157. *Cheilodipterus lachneri* (Klausewitz). The alternating dark and darker stripes and the yellow around the tail spot make identification of this species easier. Photo by Dr. Herbert R. Axelrod. Maldives.

158. *Archamia fucata* (Cantor). This 1.75-inch fish has a noticeable black spot at the base of its tail. Photo by Ray Allard. Mombasa.

159. *Archamia fucata* (Cantor). Although this fish is larger (2.28 inches) the lack of a black spot does not mean that the spot fades with age. It apparently is a case of individual variation and may appear on fishes as large as this one. Photo by Ray Allard. Mombasa.

160. *Paramia quinquelineata* (Cuvier & Valenciennes). This striped species does not belong to the same genus as the previous species. Photo of a 3.2-inch specimen by Ray Allard. Mombasa.

161. *Fowleria aurita* (Cuvier & Valenciennes). Not all cardinalfishes are red. This mottled species is very different from the ones aquarists are most familiar with. Photo by Ray Allard. Mombasa.

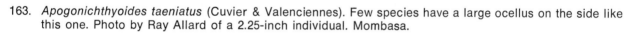

162. *Pristiapogon snyderi* (Jordan & Evermann). This cardinalfish is found all the way to the Hawaiian Islands in the Pacific Ocean. Photo of a 2-inch specimen by Ray Allard. Mombasa.

163. *Apogonichthyoides taeniatus* (Cuvier & Valenciennes). Few species have a large ocellus on the side like this one. Photo by Ray Allard of a 2.25-inch individual. Mombasa.

cies are deep water forms and are not likely to be seen by the aquarist. The enlarged canines would lead one to believe that it would be wise not to trust these fishes with smaller fishes in an aquarium.

Although scientists distinguish their species on the basis of proportional measurements, fin ray counts, gill raker counts and serrations on various bones, etc., as well as color pattern, aquarists must depend almost entirely on the coloration when trying to identify their live animals. Some of

important. In such species as *Pristiapogon snyderi* (or *Apogon snyderi* if you wish) the placement of the spot in relation to the lateral line or center line and the width and extent of the lateral band are used for identification. Unfortunately in some species the peduncular spot is variable and may be absent in some individuals of the same species, as is seen in the photos of *Archamia fucata*. The banding pattern of several cardinalfishes is useful, especially when differing numbers of bands are present (i.e. 5 in one

164. *Ostorhinchus endekataenia* (Bleeker). This species is also found in the Pacific Ocean. Photo of a 2-inch specimen by Ray Allard. Mombasa.

these color characteristics are minute, and it takes a good eye to discern the differences. In the photos of *Apogon savayensis* and *A. nubilis* on these pages the two species look very much alike. But the brownish streak below the eye is different, one being broader and extending to the eye itself, the other narrower and stopping just before the eye. In some instances the spot on the caudal peduncle is used as an identifying characteristic. Its size, shape, and position are

species and 8 in another), although it becomes less useful when comparative widths of the bands are diagnostic (except when very evident as in species like *Cheilodipterus lachneri*).

It is evident from the photos of cardinalfishes shown here that not all of them bear the red color implied by their common name. There are red cardinalfishes in the area covered, but we have been unable to secure photos of them at this time.

165. *Ostorhinchus* sp. (possibly *O. angustatus).* Cardinalfishes are mostly nocturnal, hiding among the coral and rocks during the day. Photo by Dr. Herbert R. **Axelrod.** Maldives.

166. *Ostorhinchus endekataenia (Bleeker).* Note the difference in coloration of the dorsal fins between this individual and the one on the opposite page. Photo by Dr. Herbert R. Axelrod. Maldives.

167a. Many different fishes can be found at a cleaning station. Here *Labroides dimidiatus* work over the emperor angelfish and a species of soldierfish. Photo by Rodney Jonklaas. Ceylon.

Family HOLOCENTRIDAE
SQUIRRELFISHES

Squirrelfishes are kept in home aquaria from time to time, although they are not too commonly available at pet shops. They are usually fairly active, especially during evening or early morning hours, but may stay hidden during the brightest part of the day. They are relatively attractive with red colors accented by silver and black. Some species may have some yellow coloration mixed in as well.

Of the three common genera lacking the large preopercular spine (see accompanying photos) genus *Myripristis* is the most common. It differs from *Holotrachys* in having 10 or eleven dorsal fin spines, the last longer than the penultimate and form-ing part of the soft dorsal fin. *Holotrachys* has twelve dorsal fin spines, the last approximately equal to the next to last. *Ostichthys* can be separated from *Myripristis* on scale counts, having fewer (25-35) than *Myripristis* (about 35-40).

The three genera that have the strong preopercular spine, *Flammeo, Holocentrus* and *Adioryx*, are more difficult to tell apart. *Flammeo* and *Adioryx* differ in the connection (or lack of one) between the two parts of the dorsal fin. *Flammeo* has the last spine of the dorsal fin attached to the first ray by a membrane (sometimes you have to look very close to see this) whereas there is a slight gap between the fins in *Adioryx*. *Holocentrus* has the membranous connection but has more gill rakers (14-17 on lower limb of first arch) than either of the other two genera (11-13 on lower limb of first arch).

167. *Adioryx spinifer* (Forskal). This species is often found in caves or holes during the day. Photo by Dr. Herbert R. Axelrod. Maldives.

168. *Adioryx spinifer* (Forskal). At cleaning time (notice the cleaner wrasse below the pelvic fin) the long-jawed squirrelfish may venture out of its cave. Photo by Rodney Jonklaas. Ceylon.

169. *Adioryx andamanensis* (Day). Large eyes are necessary for better vision in dark caves or at night. These fishes avoid bright light. Photo by Dr. Herbert R. Axelrod. Maldives.

170. *Adioryx caudimaculatus* (Ruppell). The bright spot on the caudal peduncle near the base of the dorsal fin is an identifying characteristic. Photo by Ray Allard. Mombasa.

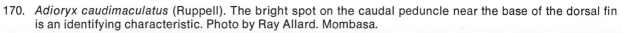

171. *Adioryx spinifer* (Forskal). Poking into a cave like this, one will often turn up several species of squirrel-fishes. Photo by Rodney Jonklaas. Ceylon.

692

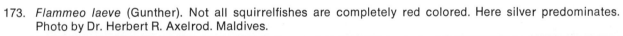

172. *Adioryx lacteoguttatus* (Cuvier). This Indo-Pacific species attains a length of some 9 inches. Photo by Dr. Herbert R. Axelrod. Maldives.

173. *Flammeo laeve* (Gunther). Not all squirrelfishes are completely red colored. Here silver predominates. Photo by Dr. Herbert R. Axelrod. Maldives.

174. *Myripristis violaceous* (Bleeker). Soldierfishes do very well in the marine aquarium. Photo by Ray Allard. Mombasa.

175. *Myripristis pralinus* Cuvier. Notice the interruption of the black band from opercle to pectoral fin. Photo by Dr. Herbert R. Axelrod. Maldives.

176. *Priacanthus hamrur* (Forskal). (Family Priacanthidae) The lunate caudal fin provides a clue to the identity of this species. Photo by Dr. Herbert R. Axelrod. Maldives.

177. *Priacanthus hamrur* (Forskal). This fish became a pet of one of the authors (HRA). The fish followed him as he swam about the reefs taking photos. Photo by Dr. Herbert R. Axelrod. Maldives.

178. Even a young barracuda *(Sphyraena japonica?)* is a predator to be reckoned with. Photo by Dr. Herbert R. Axelrod. Mombasa.

179. *Pempheris schwenki* Bleeker. Sweepers are usually seen in schools. Photo by Ray Allard. Mombasa.

180. *Corythoichthys intestinalis* (Ramsay). The head of the pipefish is similar to that of the related sea horses. Photo by Dr. Herbert R. Axelrod. Maldives.

181. *Corythoichthys intestinalis* (Ramsay). The body is encased in hard modified scales and is angular in cross section. Photo by Dr. Herbert R. Axelrod. Maldives.

182. The combination of *Dascyllus* and *Chromis* species around a head of coral is a common underwater sight. Photo by Dr. Herbert R. Axelrod. Maldives.

Family POMACENTRIDAE
DAMSELFISHES AND ANEMONEFISHES

In preparing the photos for this third book of *Pacific Marine Fishes* one of the species of the genus *Dascyllus* was tentatively identified as *Dascyllus reticulatus*. Upon closer scrutiny, however, differences between the fish pictured and the true *Dascyllus reticulatus* became evident and a search for the proper name began. It appears that *Dascyllus carneus* was used for this species and it is that name that will be used here. In comparison with *D. reticulatus* (#364, p. 205) *carneus* has a blue dorsal fin, blue spots on the head and chest and blue markings on the body scales, and a white caudal peduncle along with the caudal fin. The remaining pattern and colors seem to be similar probably indicating a very close relationship between the two.

Another fish was photographed that looked like a species of *Dascyllus* but actually was a species of *Abudefduf*. The *Dascyllus* and *Abudefduf* photos are placed on the same page so that the similarities (and differences) can be seen at a glance. The *Dascyllus* (#231, p. 738) not only has a different color pattern but has the typical steeper more blunt head profile than does the *Abudefduf* (#232, p. 738).

Two species of anemonefishes that were not illustrated in color in our book *Anemonefishes,* by Dr. Gerald R. Allen, were finally photographed. *Amphiprion allardi*, which was named by Dr. Klausewitz of the Senckenberg Museum, Germany, after Ray Allard, was taken in Mombasa. *Amphiprion nigripes* was photographed for the first time in the Maldives, apparently the only place it has ever been found. Neither species should be readily available to American aquarists because of the shipping distances involved, but both turn up in European markets. It is interesting to note that the head band of *Amphiprion nigripes* is quite variable, being broad in one indi-

701

183. *Dascyllus aruanus* (Linnaeus). One of the most popular aquarium fishes, this species is very hardy and is always available. Photo by Dr. Herbert R. Axelrod. Maldives.

184. *Dascyllus carneus* (Fischer). This species may be identical with *D. reticulatus* but differs in some aspects of the color pattern (see p. 205 #364). Photo by Ray Allard. Mombasa.

185. *Dascyllus carneus* (Fischer). The blue dorsal fin, blue spots on the head, and the white caudal peduncle all are characteristics of *D. carneus* not found in *D. reticulatus.* Photo by U. Erich Friese. Mombasa.

186. *Amphiprion clarkii* (Bennett). The two-banded anemonefish most often seen in pet shops and aquarium stores is this species. Photo by Dr. Herbert R. Axelrod. Maldives.

187. *Amphiprion allardi* Klausewitz. A pair of Allard's
clownfishes standing guard over their eggs (yellow objects to the lower right). Photo by D. Terver,
Nancy Aquarium, France.

188. *Amphiprion* species. Nestled in the safety of its anemone this fish almost dares predators to try and capture it. Photo by Dr. Herbert R. Axelrod.

189. A little nip at the tentacles of the anemone may
     have something to do with continuing immuniza-
     tion from its stinging cells or, possibly, the fish
     actually eats it. Photo by Dr. Herbert R. Axelrod.

190. *Amphiprion clarkii* (Bennett). This species is similar in color pattern to the one below but differs as can be seen. Photo by Dr. Herbert R. Axelrod. Maldives.

191. *Amphiprion allardi* Klausewitz. One of our photographers, Ray Allard, had this anemonefish named in his honor. Photo by Dr. Herbert R. Axelrod. Mombasa.

192. *Amphiprion clarkii* (Bennett). In its natural habitat an anemone may settle in a hole so that only the tentacles stick out. Photo by Rodney Jonklaas, Ceylon.

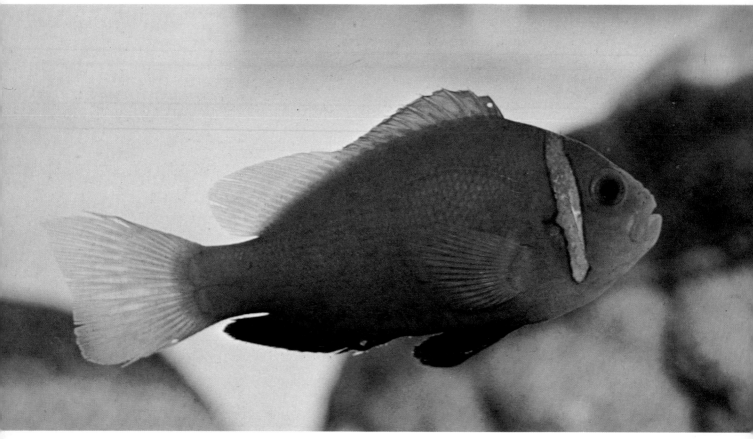

193. *Amphiprion nigripes* Regan. The specific name of this fish refers to the black anal and pelvic fins. Photo by Dr. Herbert R. Axelrod. Maldives.

194. *Amphiprion nigripes* Regan. Because of its very limited distribution (only in the Maldive Islands), the black-finned anemonefish may not be seen in the aquarium trade. Photo by Dr. Herbert R. Axelrod. Maldives.

195. *Amphiprion nigripes* Regan. This pair of fish looks very much like skunk clownfish but the dark pelvic and anal fins tip us off that they are not. Photo by Rodney Jonklaas. Maldives.

196. *Amphiprion nigripes* Regan. The varying widths of the head band can be seen in this and previous photos. Here it is very narrow. Photo by Dr. Herbert R. Axelrod. Maldives.

197. *Amphiprion nigripes* Regan. A whole colony of anemonefishes sharing an anemone or two. Photo by Rodney Jonklaas.

198. *Amphiprion nigripes* Regan. The black-finned anemonefish seems to be sharing the anemone with *Amphiprion clarkii* (lower left) and *Dascyllus trimaculatus* (lower right). Photo by Dr. Herbert R. Axelrod. Maldives.

714

199. *Amphiprion clarkii* (Bennett). Usually a pair of anemonefish will set up their territory around a single anemone. Photo by Dr. Herbert R. Axelrod. Maldives.

200. *Lepidozygus anthioides* Smith. One of the more unusual damselfishes, rarely seen in aquaria. Photo by Dr. Herbert R. Axelrod. Maldives.

vidual and extremely narrow in another. We are happy to present these fishes to you not only in a close-up diagnostic photo but in their natural habitat as well.

Also presented for the first time is the genus *Lepidozygus*. Its physiognomy is quite different from most of the pomacentrid genera being quite elongate in comparison. They seem to approach genus *Chromis* most closely.

There are some species included here which have not as yet been identified. Current research on this family is underway and it is hoped that we may soon have the proper names of these fishes. Several fishes presented here are shown in various color patterns. However, it can be seen from the photos that one can merge into another with very little effort. Normally black markings such as spots are useful in identification of these fishes, but care should be taken as in some species they are variable in intensity (though usually constant in position).

One species, *Abudefduf sordidus,* appears to have been caught guarding a nest placed on a piling. The sequence of photos presented were taken to depict the care the parent fish will give to the nest. The piling was not approached too closely for fear of disturbing the fish so much that it might eat the eggs, as has been known to happen in such circumstances.

201. *Lepidozygus anthioides* Smith. A darker phase of the same species from the African coast. Photo by Ray Allard. Mombasa.

202. *Chromis dimidiatus* (Klunzinger). This dark and light colored damselfish is a member of a species complex of similar patterns. Photo by Ray Allard. Mombasa.

203. *Chromis ternatensis* (Bleeker). The slender peduncle and forked tail give this damsel a more streamlined appearance than other damsels. Photo by Dr. Herbert R. Axelrod. Maldives.

204. *Pomacentrus nigricans* (Lacepede). Damselfishes are highly territorial. This one may not tolerate the presence of the lizardfish (center of photo). Photo by Rodney Jonklaas. Ceylon.

205. Unidentified young damselfish from the Maldives. Photo by Dr. Herbert R. Axelrod.

207. *Pomacentrus* species (possibly *P. melanochir* Bleeker). Photo by Dr. Herbert R. Axelrod. Maldives.

206. *Pomacentrus nigricans* (Lacepede). The dark spots at the bases of the fins help identify damselfishes. Photo by Ray Allard, Mombasa.

209. *Pomacentrus tripunctatus* (Cuvier & Valenciennes). The darker color pattern makes this individual look different from the other two. Photo by Ray Allard. Mombasa.

208. *Pomacentrus tripunctatus* (Cuvier & Valenciennes). A small pleasingly colored damselfish that would be a nice addition to a marine aquarium. Photo by Ray Allard. Mombasa.

210. *Pomacentrus tripunctatus* (Cuvier & Valenciennes). The spot in the dorsal fin has all but disappeared, otherwise it is almost identical to the one on the opposite page. Photo by Ray Allard. Mombasa.

211. *Pomacentrus taeniurus* Bleeker. This species is found in both the Pacific and Indian Oceans. Photo by Ray Allard. Mombasa.

212. *Pomacentrus taeniurus* Bleeker. Notice the variation in the amount of yellow in the fins. Photo by Ray Allard. Mombasa.

213. *Pomacentrus pavo* (Bloch). This distinctively patterned damselfish resembles *P. taeniurus* and is closely related to it. Photo by Ray Allard. Mombasa.

214. *Pomacentrus* species (possibly *P. trichourus).* The light stripe in the dorsal fin can be seen in several dark-colored species such as this one. Photo by Dr. Herbert R. Axelrod. Maldives.

215. *Pomacentrus pulcherrimus* Smith. This beautiful species would brighten any aquarium. The yellow is somewhat variable in extent. Photo by Dr. Herbert R. Axelrod. Maldives.

216. *Abudefduf sordidus* (Forskal). Pomacentrids seek out a hard object upon which to deposit their eggs. The pilings may provide just the surface needed. Photo by Dr. Herbert R. Axelrod. Maldives.

217. *Abudefduf sordidus* (Forskal). The site of the nest is vigorously protected against all comers. The parent will not stray very far from it. Photo by Dr. Herbert R. Axelrod. Maldives.

218. *Abudefduf sordidus* (Forskal). The piling also serves as a browsing area where algae and small invertebrates can be found. Photo by Dr. Herbert R. Axelrod. Maldives.

219. *Abudefduf dickii* (Linnaeus). The notch out of the anal fin may have been taken out by a predator. Photo by Dr. Herbert R. Axelrod. Mombasa.

220. *Abudefduf lacrymatus* (Quoy and Gaimard). The pattern of blue spots reminds one of the jewel fish of the Caribbean. Photo by Dr. Herbert R. Axelrod. Maldives.

731

221. & 222. *Abudefduf biocellatus* (Quoy & Gaimard). This highly variable species is shown in four of its various color combinations. Photo above by Dr. Herbert R. Axelrod-Maldives; lower photo by Ray Allard-Mombasa.

223. & 224. *Abudefduf biocellatus* (Quoy & Gaimard). These individuals show a little more of the brilliant blue markings that may appear. Photo above by Dr. Herbert R. Axelrod-Maldives; photo below by Dr. Herbert R. Axelrod-Maldives.

225. *Abudefduf glaucus* (Cuvier & Valenciennes). The range of this species is large, being found from the coast of Africa to the Pacific Ocean. Photo by Ray Allard. Mombasa.

226. *Abudefduf lacrymatus* (Quoy & Gaimard). A combination of lighting and basic color difference contributed to the variation of color between these two photos. Photo by Ray Allard. Mombasa.

227. *Abudefduf lacrymatus* (Quoy & Gaimard). In both photos the blue spots that identify this species are distinct. Photo by Dr. Herbert R. Axelrod. Maldives.

228. *Abudefduf sexfasciatus* (Lacepede). There are many barred species of the genus *Abudefduf*. The caudal pattern helps to identify this one. Photo by Ray Allard. Mombasa.

229. *Abudefduf sparoides* (Cuvier & Valenciennes). Apparently this species is restricted to the area of the western Indian Ocean. Photo by Ray Allard. Mombasa.

230. *Abudefduf vaigiensis* (Quoy & Gaimard). This species is often considered the same as *A. saxatilis* a very wide ranging species. Photo by Dr. Herbert R. Axelrod. Maldives.

231. *Dascyllus aruanus* (Linnaeus). One of the commonest aquarium fishes, the black and white striped pattern is familiar to most marine aquarists. Photo by Ray Allard. Mombasa.

232. *Abudefduf annulatus* (Peters). This *Abudefduf* species looks very much like a species of *Dascyllus* with its similar barred pattern. Photo by Ray Allard. Mombasa.

Family MULLIDAE
GOATFISHES

Goatfishes, or surmullets as they are sometimes called, are often kept in marine aquaria. They are hardy fishes that constantly forage on the bottom with their sensory barbels. This causes problems if very fine bottom material is used. The goatfishes would keep it constantly stirred up, giving the tank a cloudy appearance. On the plus side, bits of food that have fallen to the bottom and are not touched by other fishes in the tank are usually snatched up by the goatfishes.

Identification of these fishes can be made on the basis of color, though several closely related forms might give the novice some trouble. Genera are more difficult to distinguish. *Upeneus* is differentiated from *Pseudupeneus*, *Parupeneus*, and *Mulloidichthys* by having teeth on the palate (vomerine and palatine bones) which are absent in the latter genera. *Mulloidichthys* has small jaw teeth in several rows anteriorly (forming a villiform band), *Pseudupeneus* has two rows of teeth anteriorly, and *Parupeneus* has a single row of large, blunt-tipped teeth. The aquarist therefore cannot examine his live specimens for tooth characteristics and must rely on color pattern alone. As noted in book 1 (p. 259) goatfishes have the ability to change their color patterns. This is clearly shown in the accompanying photographs of *Pseudupeneus macronema*. It was thought that *Pseudupeneus chryseredros* and *P. cyclostomas* are one and the same species. Although very close there are certain distinctions that appear that cause some doubt as to this position; they are considered here as separate species.

233. *Mulloidichthys samoensis* Gunther. Goatfishes will help pick up uneaten food from the sand or gravel of your aquarium. Photo by Dr. Herbert R. Axelrod. Maldives.

234. *Pseudupeneus chryseredros* (Lacepede). The golden saddle behind the second dorsal fin is diagnostic. Photo by Ray Allard. Mombasa.

235. *Pseudupeneus cyclostomus* (Lacepede). This species and the one above are often considered the same. Photo by Ray Allard. Mombasa.

236. *Pseudupeneus macronema* (Lacepede). The pale or blotchy phase of this species has much less red than that phase shown below. Photo by Ray Allard. Mombasa.

237. *Pseudupeneus macronema* (Lacepede). The blue lines below the eyes are found in several species of goatfishes. Photo by Dr. Herbert R. Axelrod. Mombasa.

238. Schools of *Caesio* and *Anthias* add color to the Indian Ocean reefs. Photo by Rodney Jonklaas. Maldives.

Family CHAETODONTIDAE
BUTTERFLYFISHES

Most of the butterflyfishes found across the Indian Ocean are present in the Pacific Ocean as well. However, there are several species that occur only in the Indian Ocean and vicinity. One of these, *Chaetodon xanthocephalus,* is shown in the photographs, but unfortunately will rarely be seen by American aquarists unless their local dealers have contacts that permit them to import fishes from Ceylon or other Indian Ocean shippers. *Chaetodon kleini* on the other hand is very widespread and extends from the African coast all the way to the islands of the Pacific. In most areas it is relatively common. It appears on the market from time to time but due to its less spectacular colors when compared with many other butterflyfishes it is overlooked much of the time.

The butterflyfish genera are relatively easy to distinguish. *Forcipiger* is well known among aquarists because of its prolonged snout. Its recent name change to *Forcipiger flavissimus* (a *Forcipiger longirostris* exists though it is a rare species) is finally gaining

239. *Chaetodon triangulum* Cuvier & Valenciennes. The chevron pattern occurs in a few species of butterfly-fishes. Photo by Dr. Herbert R. Axelrod. Maldives.

240. *Chaetodon kleinii* Bloch. Probably the most confused of the butterflyfishes with many different names applied to it at one time or another. Photo by Dr. Herbert R. Axelrod. Maldives.

241. *Chaetodon kleinii* Bloch. Butterflyfishes always seem to be inspecting the coral for small bits to eat. Photo by Rodney Jonklaas. Ceylon.

243. *Chaetodon xanthocephalus* Bennett. This butter-flyfish will be imported to the United States only rarely since it has to be transported all the way from the Indian Ocean. Photo by Dr. Herbert R. Axelrod. Maldives.

242. *Chaetodon xanthocephalus* Bennett. The last remnants of the eye band can be seen in this head shot. Photo by Dr. Herbert R. Axelrod. Maldives.

244. *Chaetodon bennetti* Cuvier & Valenciennes. Bennett's butterflyfish was named after the scientist who described the previous species. Photo by Rodney Jonklaas. Ceylon.

245. *Chaetodon auriga* Forskal. The juvenile differs but little from the adult. The filament grows as the fish grows. Photo by Dr. Herbert R. Axelrod. Maldives.

246. *Chaetodon auriga* Forskal. The adult differs in some slight aspects of the color pattern such as the width of the eye band. Photo by Dr. Herbert R. Axelrod. Maldives.

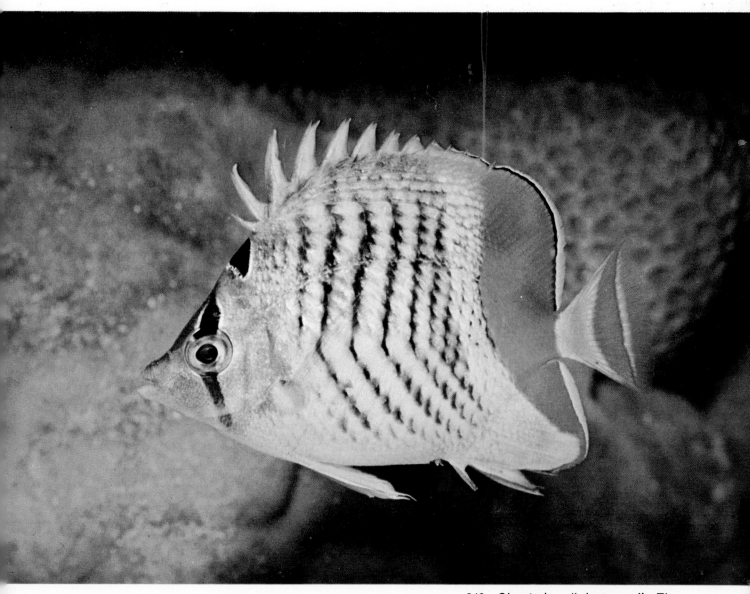

248. *Chaetodon "chrysurus".* The name of this fish is incorrect and will eventually be changed, hence the parentheses. Photo by Dr. Herbert R. Axelrod. Maldives.

247. *Chaetodon "chrysurus".* Notice the differing shades of color of the orange posterior depending upon the lighting. Photo by Rodney Jonklaas. Ceylon.

249. *Chaetodon melanotus* Bloch & Schneider. The sides of this fish will be brilliant white with black stripes when it is in the best of shape. Photo by Dr. Herbert R. Axelrod. Maldives.

250. *Chaetodon guttatissimus* Bennett. The orange-yellow edge of the dorsal fin's last rays may become bright red-orange. Photo by Dr. Herbert R. Axelrod. Maldives.

251. *Chaetodon guttatissimus* Bennett. Butterflyfishes usually travel in pairs such as these two. Photo by Dr. Herbert R. Axelrod. Maldives.

252. *Chaetodon semeion* Bleeker. Although found in both Pacific and Indian Oceans, the golden butterflyfish is never common. Photo by Rodney Jonklaas. Ceylon.

255. *Chaetodon meyeri* Bloch & Schneider. Meyer's butterflyfish has a complicated pattern of head stripes. Photo by Dr. Herbert R. Axelrod. Maldives.

256. The companion to this
Chaetodon meyeri should be
close by. Photo by Rodney
Jonklaas. Ceylon.

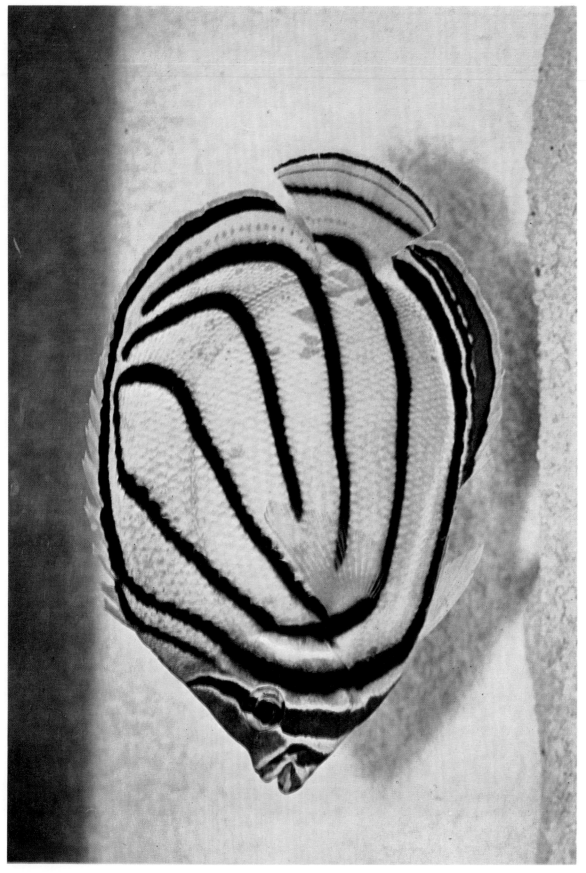

257. *Chaetodon meyeri* Bloch & Schneider. The lined pattern makes Meyer's butterflyfish easy to identify. Photo by Dr. Herbert R. Axelrod. Maldives.

258. *Chaetodon falcula* Bloch. The eye band here almost completely obscures the eye. Photo by Dr. Herbert R. Axelrod. Maldives.

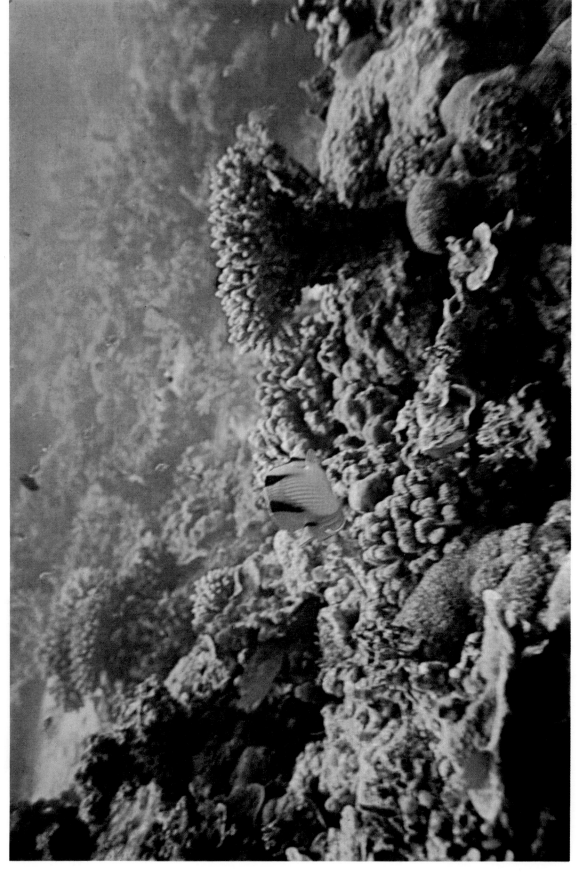

259. This butterflyfish, *Chaetodon falcula*, stands out on a coral reef. The fishes in the background are *Anthias* sp. Photo by Rodney Jonklaas. Ceylon.

acceptance in the aquarium trade. This process is necessarily slow since it is usually difficult for us to break a long-standing habit. The other long-snouted butterflyfish genus, *Chelmon,* with *Chelmon rostratus* being one of the most popular of butterflyfishes. It is known in the trade as the copperband or coral butterflyfish and has been reported from the Indian Ocean although the center of its distribution seems to be around southeast Asia.

The genus *Heniochus* contains about seven species, all having a generally similar appearance with the fourth dorsal fin spine prominently elongated. *Heniochus acuminatus* carries this to an extreme where the filament of the spine is as long as the body or even longer. In *Heniochus pleurotaenia* shown here the fourth dorsal fin spine is much shorter.

The largest genus of butterflyfishes is the genus *Chaetodon,* with almost ninety species. They vary quite a bit in shape from one species to another but they are usually easily recognizable as butterflyfishes. Some, like *Chaetodon auriga,* have one or more rays of the dorsal fin extended into a filament. There has been no theory advanced as to what possible purpose or use this might be for the fish other than a species recognition signal. *Chaetodon semeion,* like *Chaetodon auriga,* has a filament in the dorsal fin but it is less well developed and projects from a more rounded fin.

260. *Chaetodon falcula* is rather shy, and an underwater photographer has a difficult time getting it to pose properly. Photo by Dr. Herbert R. Axelrod. Maldives.

262. *Chaetodon pictus.*
Forskal. This species is
occasionally imported from
Ceylon. Photo by Dr.
Herbert R. Axelrod.
Maldives.

261. *Chaetodon plebeius*
(Cuvier & Valenciennes).
The lateral spot in this
specimen has faded out,
probably due to fright while
having his photograph
taken. Photo by Rodney
Jonklaas. Ceylon.

263. *Chaetodon lineolatus* Cuvier. The lined butterflyfish is the largest of the butterflyfishes, growing to over a foot in length. Photo by Dr. Herbert R. Axelrod. Maldives.

264. *Chaetodon lineolatus* Cuvier. A field of stagshorn coral (*Acropora*) provides hiding places for many fishes such as this butterflyfish. Photo by Dr. Herbert R. Axelrod. Maldives.

Chaetodon falcula has a rather projecting snout but far from the slender, elongate ones of *Forcipiger* and *Chelmon*. The photos of *Chaetodon falcula* presented here in its natural habitat might be misleading for a single individual of a butterflyfish is not often seen, a second one is usually not far away. A typical pair of butterflyfishes is seen in the photograph of *Chaetodon guttatissimus* (#251).

The reef is definitely the home of the butterflyfish as can be seen in almost every underwater photo of these fishes. It has been stated by AHL (1933) that butterflyfishes appear on every coral reef in the world. If no butterflyfish has been reported from a particular reef it only means that the collecting has not been thorough enough.

Several species of butterflyfishes have recently been kept in marine aquaria successfully for long periods of time (5 years or more). With the appearance of some of the new packaged marine fish foods their survival in captivity becomes more and more assured. Not only have items such as squid and clams been packaged but the addition of vegetable matter (usually kelp) adds something to their diet that was apparently lacking previously.

266. *Heniochus varius* (Cuvier).
A species closely related to
Heniochus pleurotaenia. Photo by
Dr. Herbert R. Axelrod. Maldives.

265. *Heniochus pleurotaenia* Ahl. A whole school of this species browsing among the different species of coral. Photo by Rodney Jonklaas. Ceylon.

267. *Heniochus pleurotaenia* Ahl. In this and the above species the bony projection on the nape is well developed. Photo by Dr. Herbert R. Axelrod. Maldives

268. *Hemitaurichthys zoster* (Bennett). Note the difference between this species and *Hemitaurichthys polylepis* (p. 41). Photo by Dr. Herbert R. Axelrod. Maldives.

269. *Hemitaurichthys zoster* (Bennett). Looking straight down on a school of *Hemitaurichthys*. Photo by Dr. Herbert R. Axelrod. Maldives.

270. *Forcipiger flavissimus* Jordan & McGregor. From Hawaii to the African coast the long-nosed butterflyfish appear identical. Photo by Dr. Herbert R. Axelrod. Maldives.

271. *Gerres oyena* (Forskal).
This species frequents coastal
areas especially bays and the
mouths of rivers. Photo by
Ray Allard. Mombasa.

272. *Aulostomus chinensis* (Linnaeus). The fin structure of this fish is quite different from that of the "normal" fish as can be seen in this photo. Photo by Dr. Herbert R. Axelrod. Maldives.

273. *Aulostomus chinensis* (Linnaeus). This fish may hover vertically near sea grasses or sea whips only to dart out when a small unsuspecting fish swims by. Photo by Dr. Herbert R. Axelrod. Maldives.

Family AULOSTOMIDAE

TRUMPETFISHES

The trumpetfishes are elongate, compressed fishes with a small mouth at the end of the long snout. The prominent lower jaw has a small barbel at its symphysis. The soft dorsal and anal fins are posteriorly placed, with about 20 to 30 rays each, and the spinous dorsal fin is reduced to 8 to 12 isolated spines positioned anterior to the soft dorsal fin. The ventrals are abdominal in position and contain six rays. The caudal fin is rhomboidal in shape and lacks the elongate filament of the related cornetfish of the family Fistulariidae.

The trumpetfishes are moderate sized fishes reaching a length of about two feet or more. They inhabit reef areas in tropical oceans of the world. Often they may be seen swimming in shallow water at or near the surface, or standing perpendicularly in the water, usually around branching coral or algal fronds. Their capacity to change colors to match these surroundings is quite extraordinary and trumpetfishes are not often seen until some movement gives them away. This movement usually denotes the disappearance of some small fish that has approached the area where the trumpetfish was waiting. The color patterns not only can change from a yellow to red or brown but often bars or horizontal lines will appear.

The trumpetfishes have been observed and photographed lying horizontally alongside large fishes much like a *Remora* would do. This association is quite odd and theories concerning the possible reasons behind it include camouflage, in which the trumpetfish will suddenly dart out from its host to capture an unsuspecting fish, or transportation, in which the trumpetfish will "hop on" a large fish that is passing by such as an adult parrotfish, to be able to move about the reef more rapidly at the expense of the larger fishes energy. And of course there might be a combination of the two reasons.

274. *Synodus indicus* (Day) and *Pomacentrus nigricans* Lacepede confronting each other, possibly over a disputed territory. Photo by Rodney Jonklaas. Ceylon.

275. *Platycephalus* sp. (possibly *P. grandidieri* Sauvage). Some species of this genus attain lengths of almost two feet. Photo by Ray Allard. Mombasa.

276. *Platycephalus* sp. (possibly *P. grandidieri* Sauvage). The side view above and the top view here show why these fishes are called flatheads. Photo by Ray Allard. Mombasa.

277. *Parapercis cylindrica* (Bloch). The male of this species has narrow lines on the head as shown here. This is also the typical pose of a mugiloid. Photo by Dr. Herbert R. Axelrod. Maldives.

Family MUGILOIDIDAE (PARAPERCIDAE)
WEEVERS

In keeping with the most recently proposed classification of fishes, we have changed the name of the family of weevers from Parapercidae (which was used in Book 2, p. 467) to Mugiloididae. Although Parapercidae is still used by some well-known ichthyologists, we decided to follow the latest word on fish systematics. The name Parapercidae is included in parentheses to avoid giving the impression that we are dealing with a different family altogether.

The genus *Parapercis* is the largest genus (in numbers) in the family. Aside from characteristics which the aquarist cannot use such as number of gill rakers or scales along the lateral line, the color pattern figures prominently in the identification of these fishes. Like many other fishes there are some problems in distinguishing the species by color alone. Apparently males and females have some aspects of the color pattern diffcrent from each other. In the species shown, the male of *Parapercis cylindrica* has a pattern of lines on the cheek area. The female has a pattern of dots or spots. Young weevers may also differ from the adult in some aspects of the pattern. The caudal fin of the young fish pictured here is mostly dark whereas in the adult the dark area has been reduced to more or less the central rays. And of course to further complicate matters the fishes have the ability to change the pattern to some extent, exhibiting bars at one time and splotches at another. It is interesting to note that the light splotch on the caudal fin of *Parapercis cephalopunctatus* is a part of the color pattern and not a discoloration of some sort.

278. *Parapercis cylindrica* (Bloch). This young fish has spots on its head and is probably the female of the species. Photo by Dr. Herbert R. Axelrod. Maldives.

279. *Parapercis cephalopunctatus* (Seale). For bottom dwelling fishes such as this one, eyes placed on an angle give better vision upwards. Photo by Dr. Herbert R. Axelrod. Maldives.

280. *Parapercis cephalopunctatus* (Seale). The light blotch on the tail fin is a permanent fixture. Photo by Dr. Herbert R. Axelrod. Maldives.

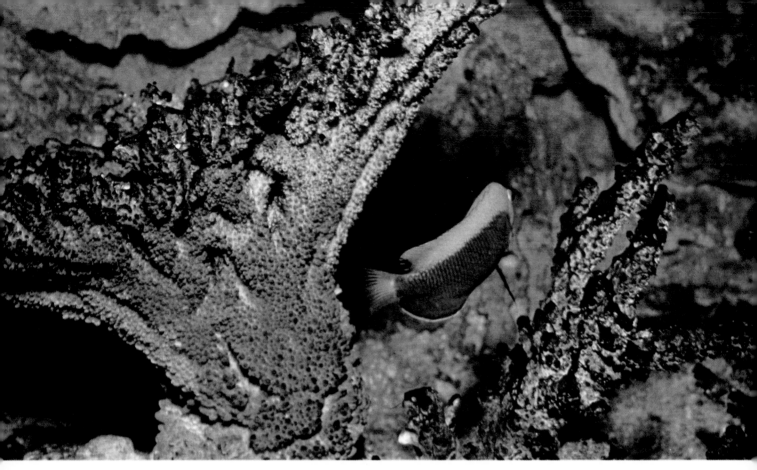

281. *Centropyge acanthops* Norman. This beautiful angelfish is rarely seen in American stores but does appear from time to time in the European markets. Photo by Dr. Herbert R. Axelrod. Mombasa.

282. *Centropyge acanthops* Norman. This fish was at one time misidentified as the Hawaiian *Centropyge fisheri* but the two are quite different. Photo by Dr. Herbert R. Axelrod. Mombasa.

Family POMACANTHIDAE
ANGELFISHES

Angelfishes, like butterflyfishes, wrasses, etc., can be identified with a fair amount of certainty by color pattern alone. Most marine aquarists are familiar with these fishes because their brilliant color patterns and pleasing body shapes have made them extremely popular fishes, and almost every shipment of marine tropicals includes some angelfish.

The genus *Centropyge* contains such favorites as the lemonpeel *(Centropyge flavissimus)*, the flame angel *(C. loriculus),* and the coral beauty *(C. bispinosus).* Although just as attractive as some of these just mentioned species, the African cherub-fish *(Centropyge acanthops)* is rarely seen in the United States. The distance from the home of this species to Europe is much less and it does appear for sale there (usually under the name *Centropyge fisheri).* The fishes of this genus are small, usually less than five inches in length, with thirteen to fifteen dorsal fin spines and regularly arranged scales on the sides. The interoperculum is small, serrated or with spines posteriorly; the hind margin of the preorbital is free, and the lateral line ends at the base of the soft dorsal fin rays.

Pomacanthus is a genus of mostly larger fishes, reaching a length of over a foot, which undergo fantastic changes in color pattern with age (see Book 1). The scales of this genus (and *Chaetodontoplus*

283. *Centropyge bispinosus* (Gunther). One of the best known small angelfishes. Photo by Dr. Herbert R. Axelrod. Maldives.

284. *Centropyge multispinus* (Playfair). This species is much less colorful than *Centropyge bispinosus,* with which it is sometimes confused. Photo by Dr. Herbert R. Axelrod. Maldives.

285. *Centropyge multispinus* (Playfair). With different lighting, the blue trim of this fish shows up very well. Photo by Rodney Jonklaas. Ceylon.

286. *Euxiphipops xanthometapon* (Bleeker). The blue-faced angelfish eyes the photographer and cautiously remains near the coral. Photo by Rodney Jonklaas. Ceylon.

287. *Apolemichthys xanthurus* (Bennett). Angelfishes can be identified by the strong preopercular spine. Photo by Dr. Herbert R. Axelrod. Maldives.

289. *Apolemichthys trimaculatus* (Lacepede). This species appears in shipments from both Ceylon and the Philippines. Photo by Dr. Herbert R. Axelrod. Maldives.

as well) are very small, irregularly placed, and number at least 70 in a lateral series. These are very difficult to count and estimates are usually made. The lateral line of genus *Pomacanthus* ends at the base of the caudal fin, that of the genus *Chaetodontoplus* reaches only to the base of the last dorsal fin rays.

Euxiphipops has a complete lateral line, regularly arranged scales, a broad interorbital space (broader than the eye diameter), and a large and entire interoperculum. Juveniles are quite different from the adults.

Pygoplites includes only a single species, *P. diacanthus,* which is easily recognized, and further distinction need not concern us at this time. The young of the regal angelfish are very similar to the adult with only minor differences in the color pattern.

The genus *Apolemichthys* is represented in the Indian Ocean by only a few species. The two shown on the preceding pages are the ones most likely to be encoun-

290. *Pomacanthus imperator* (Bloch). The fine, hair-like teeth can be seen in this photograph. Photo by Dr. Herbert R. Axelrod. Maldives.

291. *Pomacanthus imperator* (Bloch). The adult emperor angelfish may get to be about a foot and a half in length. Photo by Dr. Herbert R. Axelrod. Maldives.

tered in this area. *Apolemichthys xanthurus* would more likely be available to the European marine aquarists, but *Apolemichthys trimaculatus* is widespread and common enough to be available both in Europe and the United States.

Juveniles of many angelfishes are kept by aquarists. They soon outgrow the aquaria, however, placing the owner in a predicament: should he purchase a larger tank or dispose of the fish by giving it away? Species of the genus *Centropyge* are the exception and adults can easily be kept for years.

292. *Pomacanthus imperator* (Bloch). This large emperor angelfish is at home among the coral of the reef. Photo by Rodney Jonklaas. Ceylon.

293. *Pygoplites diacanthus* (Boddaert). One angelfish seems more spectacular than the next. The variety of color of these fishes is unlimited. Photo by Dr. Herbert R. Axelrod. Maldives.

295. *Kuhlia taeniura* (Cuvier & Valenciennes). The common name flagtail is usually applied to fishes with these black and white bars. Photo by Dr. Herbert R. Axelrod. Maldives.

294. *Pygoplites diacanthus* (Boddaert). For all its bright colors, the regal angelfish spends a lot of its time in a dark hole or cave on the reef. Photo by Dr. Herbert R. Axelrod. Maldives.

296. *Acanthurus triostegus* (Linnaeus). This species is probably the most common of the surgeonfishes. Photo by Ray Allard. Mombasa.

Family ACANTHURIDAE
SURGEONFISHES

Along with butterflyfishes, damselfishes, and wrasses, surgeonfishes are commonly seen around the coral reefs of the world. Unlike many of the families already discussed in this series the surgeonfish genera are not too difficult to tell apart. Aquarists can distinguish most genera by inspection of their living fishes.

One of the easiest to distinguish is the genus *Naso*. Many of the species of this genus have some sort of projection or bump extending from the area between the front of the dorsal fin and the mouth. There is a slender caudal peduncle provided with one to two pairs (usually two) of fixed, immovable spines. The body form is rather elongate when compared to other surgeonfishes and some species have filamentous extensions from the upper and lower edges of the caudal fin. There are four to seven stout dorsal fin spines and two strong anal fin spines. All of the predorsal projections appear in the adult stages and are useless when trying to determine the identity of the juveniles. Fin ray counts and color pattern (what there is of it) must then be used. The accompanying photos show the characteristics of these fishes very well.

297. *Acanthurus triostegus* (Linnaeus). The white ventral edge is the natural color of the convict surgeonfish, at least in the Indian Ocean. Photo by Dr. Herbert R. Axelrod. Maldives.

299. *Acanthurus tennenti* Gunther. Closely related to *Acanthurus olivaceus.* This is probably the first color photo published of the juvenile of this species. Photo by Dr. Herbert R. Axelrod. Maldives.

298. A small surgeonfish *(Acanthurus* sp.) that has apparently recently metamorphosed from its larval form. Photo by Dr. Herbert R. Axelrod. Maldives.

300. *Acanthurus gahhm* (Forskal). The dark brown "ear"-mark helps identify this species. Photo by Dr. Herbert R. Axelrod. Maldives.

301. *Acanthurus chronixis* Randall. Not only is this the first photo of the young of this species, but it is the first record of it from the Indian Ocean. The original specimen was described from the Caroline Islands. Photo by Dr. Herbert R. Axelrod. Maldives.

302. *Acanthurus leucosternon* Bennett. This brightly colored species is a favorite among marine aquarists. Photo by Dr. Herbert R. Axelrod. Maldives.

The genus *Prionurus* is probably the closest relative of the unicornfishes *(Naso)*. The body shape is similar but less elongate and there are usually three to six pairs of fixed, immovable spines posteriorly and on the caudal peduncle. Species of this genus have eight or nine strong dorsal fin spines and three anal fin spines. *Prionurus microlepidotus* has appeared in Book 1 (p. 88 #139).

Although the technical difference between the genus *Paracanthurus* and other surgeonfishes with a single movable spine on each ·side of the caudal peduncle is that *Paracanthurus* has the head scales modified to tuberculated plates, most aquarists are so familiar with the single species known, *Paracanthurus hepatus*, that further investigation is not necessary.

Species of genus *Zebrasoma* are deep bodied, giving them a more rounded appearance. This appearance is accentuated by the high dorsal and anal fins. The juveniles, which are most likely to be kept in home aquaria, have the dorsal and anal fin rays proportionately longer than the adults, giving them a greater vertical dimension than horizontal. As the fish grows this proportional relationship rapidly changes and, although the fins are still deep, the fish becomes longer than deep. Juveniles are generally similar to the adults in color pattern although some do undergo some changes. Like *Paracanthurus* there is a single movable spine on each side of the caudal peduncle. The dorsal fin contains only four or five slender spines.

The rest of the surgeonfishes are at

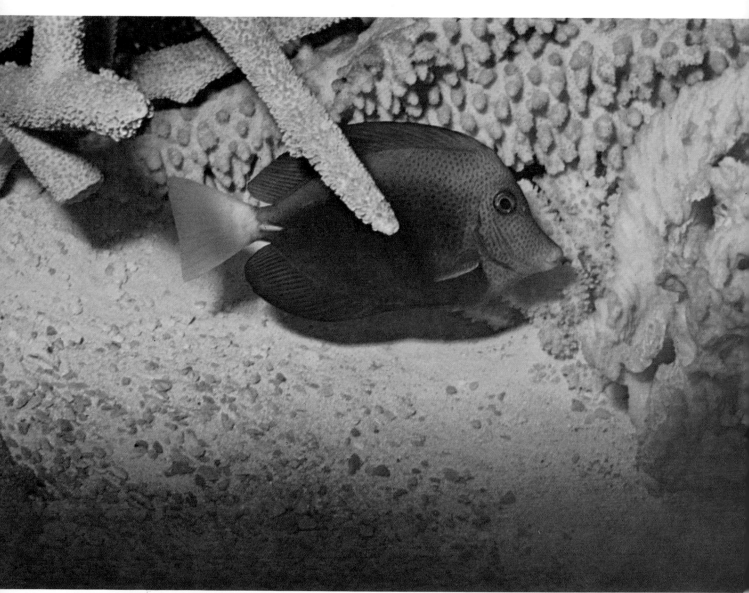

303. *Zebrasoma xanthurum* (Blyth). This species does not reach the Pacific Ocean and is only known from Ceylon to the Red Sea in the Indian Ocean. Photo by Dr. Herbert R. Axelrod.

799

306. *Zebrasoma scopas* (Cuvier). The fine pattern of small blue dots and wavy lines is barely visible in this individual. Photo by Dr. Herbert R. Axelrod. Maldives.

308. *Ctenochaetus strigosus* (Bennett). This juvenile will change considerably with age (see #198 p. 387). At least the yellow ring around the eye is constant. Photo by Dr. Herbert R. Axelrod. Maldives.

309. *Ctenochaetus striatus* (Quoy & Gaimard). Tooth characteristics are very important in distinguishing species of *Ctenochaetus*. Note the arrangement and shape of these. Photo by Dr. Herbert R. Axelrod. Maldives.

present grouped into two genera, *Acanthurus and Ctenochaetus*. These genera are more difficult to tell apart except by close inspection of the teeth. Basically the teeth of *Ctenochaetus* are movable and numerous (30 to 60 in the upper jaw) in adults. Those of genus *Acanthurus* are fixed, and there are normally less than 26 in the upper jaw. Most of the species of *Acanthurus* have nine dorsal fin spines (with only about three species having more or less spines) and species of *Ctenochaetus* normally have only eight.

The genus *Acanthurus* is the largest in the family and contains somewhat over thirty species. Most of the species have a typical body shape like that of *Acanthurus olivaceous, A. triostegus,* and *A. gahhm,* all illustrated on these pages. A few, like *Acanthurus chronixis* and *A. pyroferus,* are slightly differently shaped and appear intermediate between the basic *Acanthurus* shape mentioned and that of *Zebrasoma*.

Juveniles of most species resemble the parents in color pattern although several undergo a complete change. *Acanthurus olivaceous* for one has a bright yellow orange band behind the eye (see Book 1 p. 86).

310. *Ctenochaetus striatus* (Quoy & Gaimard). No orange ring around the eye and the presence of orange spots instead of blue spots on the head distinguish the adults of this species from *C. strigosus*. Photo by Dr. Herbert R. Axelrod. Maldives.

311. *Naso lituratus* (Bloch & Schneider). The two white areas just anterior to the eye in this head study are the openings of the nostrils. Notice the fine teeth. Photo by Dr. Herbert R. Axelrod. Maldives.

312. *Naso lituratus* (Bloch & Schneider). Most species of *Naso* are characterized in part by having more than one spine on the peduncle. Here the two spines are accented by color. Photo by Dr. Herbert R. Axelrod. Maldives.

314. *Naso unicornis* (Forskal). This individual was too large for aquarium type photography. Photo by Dr. Herbert R. Axelrod. Maldives.

313. *Naso lituratus* (Bloch & Schneider). The filaments on the tail are only present on the adult individuals. Photo by Dr. Herbert R. Axelrod. Maldives.

315. *Naso brevirostris* (Cuvier & Valenciennes). With a snout like this one, how did it ever get the name *"brevirostris?"* Photo by Dr. Herbert R. Axelrod. Maldives.

808

316. *Naso* sp. This
may be the young form
of *Naso unicornis*
(Forskal). Photo by
Ray Allard. Mombasa.

318. *Siganus stellatus* (Forskal). The spotted rabbitfish reaches a length of a little over one foot. Photo by Ray
Allard. Mombasa.

317. *Naso brevirostris*
(Cuvier & Valenci-
ennes). Juveniles such
as this one have not
developed the protub-
erance yet. Photo by
Ray Allard. Mombasa.

Family ZANCLIDAE
MOORISH IDOL

The Moorish Idol has been treated on p. 75 of Book 1. However, for this book we have been able to secure a photo of a very young individual. The differences between the young Moorish idol and the adult can be seen in the photographs on these two pages. The young individual, apparently recently metamorphosed from the pelagic "acronurus" larval stage, is depicted below (#319). It has the elongate, filamentous dorsal spine similar to that of the adult. These filaments are easily broken in handling and shipping and most of these fishes

319. *Zanclus canescens* (Linnaeus). This young specimen has a well-developed dorsal filament but the snout is still short. Photo by Ray Allard. Mombasa.

320. *Zanclus canescens* (Linnaeus). An older individual has the produced snout as well as the dorsal filament. Photo by Ray Allard. Mombasa.

offered for sale never have the magnificently developed ones seen in nature. It also seems that these filaments attract the attention of other fishes kept in the same aquarium and they nibble at them constantly, reducing them greatly in length. If left alone however, the damage is soon repaired and a new filament will grow.

The snout length also changes with age. The juvenile has a very short, stubby snout which lengthens with age to become rather prolonged. The larvae and juveniles have a different diet and apparently do not need the extension of the mouth that the adults have for foraging for food among the coral interstices or rock crevices.

The color pattern of the adult appears almost immediately after the larvae arrive on the reef. The color of the young fish shown here is almost complete, lacking only the intensity of color (the larva was transparent and silvery), and a more defined orange marking on the snout.

322. *Trachinotus bailloni* (Lacepede). Family Carangidae. This species reaches a length of about 2 feet. Photo by Dr. Herbert R. Axelrod. Maldives.

321. *Zanclus canescens* (Linnaeus). The Moorish idol is a fairly common sight on the coral reef. Usually several are seen together. Photo by Dr. Herbert R. Axelrod. Maldives.

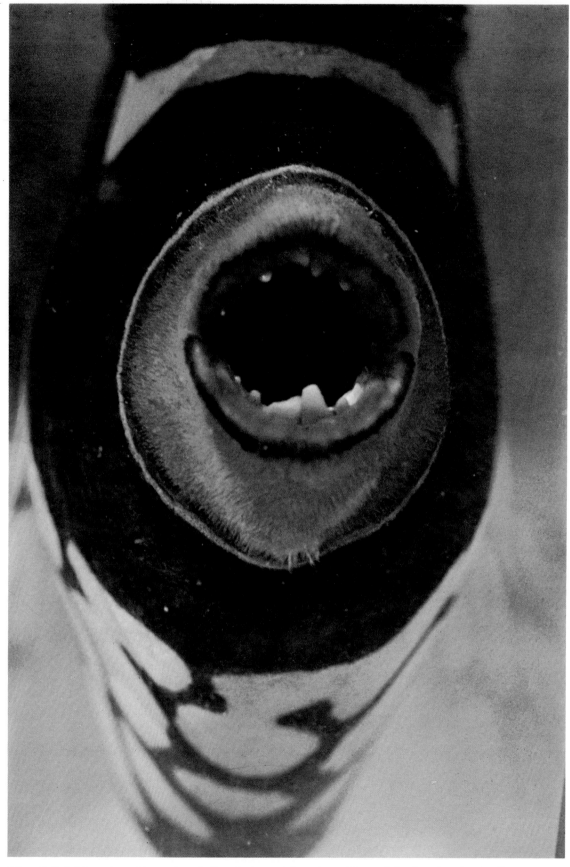

323. *Balistoides niger* (Bonnaterre). Front view of the clown triggerfish showing the tooth arrangement. Photo by Dr. Herbert R. Axelrod. Maldives.

Family BALISTIDAE
TRIGGERFISHES

There is usually no problem in identifying a triggerfish as a triggerfish. The only closely related family (and the family distinction is in great doubt) that might give one second thoughts would be the filefishes, family Monacanthidae. But the three spines of the triggerfishes as opposed to the single spine of the filefishes combined with the peculiarities of the body scalation are enough to readily separate them.

The generic distinctions are much more difficult to observe, especially on living fishes. The marine aquarist can usually recognize the species easily enough by color pattern, and generic characteristics would be sought more from curiosity than by necessity. One useful character found in such genera as *Balistoides, Sufflamen, Melichthys,* and *Pseudobalistes* but absent in *Balistapus* and *Rhinecanthus* is that the former genera possess a short, deep groove in front of each eye below the nostril. Species of *Melichthys* have teeth even and incisor-like in contrast to the uneven, notched teeth of *Sufflamen, Balistoides* (see photo), and *Pseudobalistes.* To distinguish between *Balistapus* and *Rhinecanthus,* the third spine of the dorsal fin should be examined. If it is well developed and extends beyond the edge of the groove, it is *Balistapus;* if it is minute

324. *Balistoides niger* (Bonnaterre). No triggerfish has yet been found to rival the beauty of the clown triggerfish. Photo by Dr. Herbert R. Axelrod. Maldives.

325. *Sufflamen bursa* (Bloch & Schneider). The gill openings in plectognath fishes are very small. The slit just anterior to the second vertical brown stripe behind the eye marks its position here. Photo by Dr. Herbert R. Axelrod. Maldives.

327. *Balistoides viridescens* (Bloch & Schneider). This species is rarely imported into the United States. Photo by Dr. Herbert R. Axelrod. Maldives.

328. *Balistapus undulatus* (Mungo Park). The scales are modified into a plate-like armor. Trigger-fishes feel very rough and hard. Photo by Dr. Herbert R. Axelrod. Maldives.

and hidden by the edge of the dorsal groove, it is *Rhinecanthus*.

Other characteristics defining balistid genera are the presence and arrangement of the cheek scales, tubercles on the sides of the body and peduncle, and shape of the dorsal fin.

Family MONACANTHIDAE
FILEFISHES

The filefishes, family Monacanthidae (or Aluteridae of some scientists), have been placed in with the triggerfishes, family Balistidae, in the more recent classifications. For convenience we will maintain the same classification of families that we have in Book 1. In the filefishes the dorsal fin is composed of a single large spine. However, there are remnants of a second spine which may provide a locking mechanism similar to that found in the triggerfishes.

329. *Balistapus undulatus* (Mungo Park). This pattern is found in both adults and juveniles. Photo by Dr. Herbert R. Axelrod. Maldives.

330. *Oxymonacanthus longirostris* (Bloch & Schneider). Notice that the color pattern de-emphasizes the eye but emphasizes the ventral flap. Photo by Dr. Herbert R. Axelrod. Maldives..

Differentiating the genera is a rather difficult process for the aquarist. One of the basic characteristics is whether or not there is a projecting movable spine or knob on the tip of the pelvic girdle. Even specimens available to scientists may have this portion of the fish damaged or broken, and a spine once immovable has become "movable" through rough handling. Another major characteristic is where the dorsal spine is located in relation to the eye, i.e., whether it is placed directly above the eye, somewhat behind it or in advance of it. In *Pervagor,* for instance, the spine is inserted directly above or slightly anterior to the middle of the eye. Incidentally, the spine itself may have spinules, and whether these are directed upward or downward appears to be important, as well as the ability of the spine to be depressed into a groove. The spine of *Paraluteres* cannot be fully erected and is more or less attached to the back by a flap of skin. It is without spinules and is located behind the eye. *Oxymonacanthus,* in addition to its produced snout, has a dorsal spine with spinules that is depressible into a groove.

331. *Oxymonacanthus longirostris* (Bloch & Schneider). Most marine aquarists at one time or another have seen this species for sale. Photo by Dr. Herbert R. Axelrod. Maldives.

332. *Paramonacan-thus barnardi* Fraser-Brunner. This species reaches a size of only four inches. Photo by Ray Allard. Mombasa.

333. *Cantherhines fronticinctus* (Gunther). The habitat for this species has been described as shallow water among weeds. Photo by Ray Allard. Mombasa.

Family CANTHIGASTERIDAE
SHARP-NOSED PUFFERS

The sharp-nosed puffers have been placed in the other puffers, family Tetraodontidae, in several classifications. They differ from the tetraodonts in having a more or less compressed body compared to the rounded form of the puffers, by lacking a lateral line (the puffers possess one or two lateral lines), and by the extent of the gill opening (less than halfway down the pectoral base in the sharp-nosed puffers and more than half-way down the pectoral base in the tetraodont puffers).

Additional features of the sharp-nosed puffers (though not exclusive to this family) are the single dorsal fin composed of few rays, absence of pelvic fins, parrotlike beak formed by the fusion of the teeth into two plates that are divided by a median suture, and the ability to inflate with water when disturbed.

To identify the species requires a little careful observation. The color patterns are diagnostic but there are many features which are repeated in several species. The placement and relative sizes and colors of the various stripes and spots are important. There is often a large blackish spot or blotch at the base of the dorsal fin and some sort of striping around the eyes. Incidentally, very noticeable in this group are the green eyes surrounded by an orange ring. Every one of our photos of these fishes shows this coloration.

So far only the single genus *Canthigaster* has been included in this family.

334. *Canthigaster janthinopterus* (Bleeker). This is one of the sharp-nosed puffers. Several of them have similar colored lines radiating from the eye like this one. Photo by Ray Allard. Mombasa.

335 & 336. *Paraluteres prionurus* Bleeker. An adult and juvenile filefish mimic the species of puffer shown on the opposite page. Photos of adult (above) and juvenile (below) by Ray Allard. Mombasa.

337 & 338. *Canthigaster valentini* (Bleeker). When comparing the photos of the mimic and model it is very easy to tell them apart. But underwater it is a great deal more difficult. Photos by Dr. Herbert R. Axelrod. Maldives.

339. *Canthigaster bennetti* (Bleeker). The complicated pattern of stripes and spots helps distinguish this species from others. This is the typical color. Photo by Ray Allard Mombasa.

341. *Canthigaster bennetti* (Bleeker). This individual is almost identical to the one from Mombasa on the opposite page. Photo by Dr. Herbert R. Axelrod. Maldives.

340. *Canthigaster bennetti* (Bleeker). When in its light phase the color pattern appears somewhat different. Photo by Ray Allard. Mombasa.

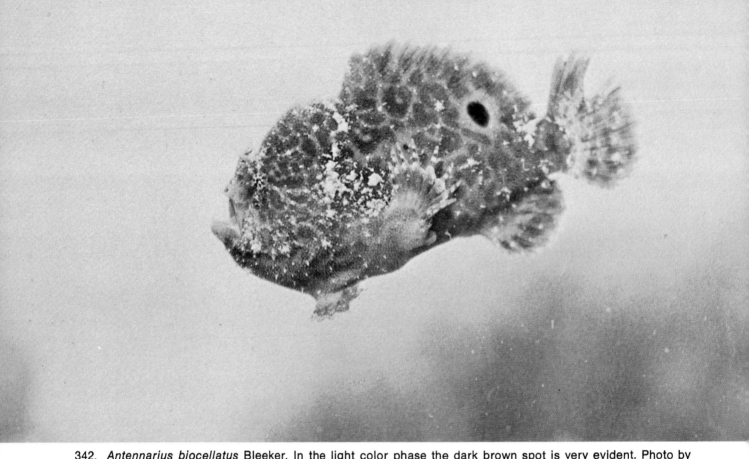

342. *Antennarius biocellatus* Bleeker. In the light color phase the dark brown spot is very evident. Photo by Ray Allard. Mombasa.

343. *Antennarius biocellatus* Bleeker. In the dark phase it is almost unnoticeable. Photo by Ray Allard. Mombasa.

INDEX

The following index contains entries for subject matter and illustrations contained in both this book and its companion volumes, *Pacific Marine Fishes* Books I and II. Some of the names used in Book I, however, have been revised to reflect an updated or otherwise changed nomenclatural standing; all such names listed in text and index of Book I are listed in this index also but are referenced to show the revised identifications.

Index

Page numbers in **bold** face refer to illustrations